HORACE

LONDON : GEOFFREY CUMBERLEGE
OXFORD UNIVERSITY PRESS

HORACE

A BIOGRAPHY

by

HENRY DWIGHT SEDGWICK

HARVARD · UNIVERSITY · PRESS

CAMBRIDGE · MASSACHUSETTS

1947

PRINTED IN THE UNITED STATES OF AMERICA

TO

R. M. S. AND F. M. S.

Aequam memento rebus in arduis servare mentem.

Horace, Odes II, III

PROLOGUE

QUINTUS HORATIUS FLACCUS! The Spirit of Civilization has placed a crown upon his head. His name has shone, and still shines, like a beacon shedding a gleam over the ocean of Time, for nearly twice a thousand years. For this there are two reasons, a lesser and a greater. The lesser is that he stands in a class alone, there is no one like him. There have been many greater poets, but none that has done what he did — take a medium so recalcitrant to lyrical use as the Latin language and compose verses that many a man of an alien nation still learns by heart, taking pleasure in their delightfulness. That was the achievement of a rare artist.

The greater reason is that the circle of his interests and sympathies turns upon the same central point as those of common humanity, and this in turn connotes many special qualities — great good sense, kind placidity, generous instincts, sensitiveness, broadmindedness.

His fame has prevailed over many enemies besides Time, *edax rerum*. It has prevailed over the death of the Latin language, over the passing of paganism, over the piety of Christianity, over multitudinous changes in the fashions of poetry, and still maintains its own against the unsympathetic currents of modern life: against the indifference of science, which values the mind of man more than his soul, against the contumely of practical men, who value neither mind nor soul but only the body.

I enter into no controversy as to the worth of the classics. I assume it, and I shall be dogmatic. These dead languages, Latin and Greek, construct a tower, like no other in the world, from which one can survey with impartiality man as a whole — body, mind, and soul — and thereby be enabled to estimate the values of life, and so separate human riches from counterfeit.

If I were to enumerate all the obstacles to the more general reading of Horace, I think I should include those learned men who are more interested in questions of scholarship than in making us see how wise, how full of common sense, how great an artist, and what a jolly good fellow Horace is; and I cannot pass in silence the unfortunate custom, for which schoolmasters are to blame since the days of Juvenal, of presenting Horace to the very young when he is essentially the poet of the middle-aged and the old. It is to those who have passed from the heat of active life into the cooler hours of the late afternoon that Horace chiefly appeals. Schoolmasters have labelled *Horace* a school book, "making a School-art of that which the Poets did only teach by a divine delightfulness," and most men have continued to regard it as such. Lord Byron and Winston Churchill are familiar instances that disclose the faults of such a method. Had Byron lived to middle age he would undoubtedly have appreciated Horace, and no one would really enjoy Horace more than Mr. Churchill, if he were ever to make acquaintance with leisure. Horace would have loved them both.

But they that value Horace most are men who, endowed by nature or taught by experience, entertain a gentle scepticism with respect to the activities of mankind: Epicureans, Cyrenaics, as well as those governed by a love of ease who prefer literature to life, or, to speak perhaps more accurately, who prefer to look at humanity and human conduct through the medium of literature.

Horace was fastitious, he was by nature an aristocrat; he did not like human beings just because they were human beings, he liked them for qualities that were pleasant to him, and men who possessed qualities unpleasant to him he did not like. The friends he loved he loved dearly, and he must have been one of the pleasantest of companions. If, on arriving at the House of Hades, Persephone should permit one to give a little stag dinner, whom out of all the glittering company would one choose? Alcibiades, Boccaccio, Chaucer, Charles d'Orléans, Voltaire, Topham Beauclerk (I am choosing my own friends), Walter Scott, Charles Lamb, Will Rogers? The list would vary according to different tastes, but to make such a dinner a complete success one most assuredly must have Horace.

My reasons for building a dinner party about Horace I shall try to make clear in this little biography.

CONTENTS

CONTENTS

HORACE

Ad Senes

Let us consider, too, how differently young and old are affected by the words of some classic author, such as . . . Horace. Passages which to a boy are but rhetorical commonplace . . . at length come home to him, when long years have passed and he has had experience of life, and pierce him, as if he had never before known them, with their sad earnestness and their vivid exactness. Then he comes to understand how it is that lines, the birth of some chance morning or evening . . . among the Sabine Hills, have lasted generation after generation, for thousands of years, with a power over the mind, and a charm, which the current literature of his own day, with all its obvious advantages, is utterly unable to rival.

John Henry Newman

I

BOYHOOD

QUINTUS HORATIUS FLACCUS was born at Venusia on December 8, 65 B.C. Venusia is a little town in southern Italy, close to the boundary between Apulia and Lucania. It lies on the Appian Way, the great highroad that ran from Rome by way of Capua and Benevento across the Apennines to Brindisi, the chief Adriatic port for Greece and the East. His father owned a little farm there near the river Aufidus and but a few miles from Mount Vultur, an extinct volcano. It was a fit place for a poet's birth; the mountain, over four thousand feet high, to a boy must have appeared of majestic height, and in the wet season the river Aufidus dashes violently down and sounds its bull-mouthed (*tauriformis*) clamor far and near (Odes III, xxx, IV, ix, xiv). In one of his odes the poet recounts what purports to be an incident of his childhood. When, tired with play, he had fallen asleep in the woods on the mountain side doves came and covered him with fresh leaves of bay and myrtle. It was indeed an extraordinary happening, and the country folk roundabout wondered that neither bear nor snake had hurt him, and explained to one another that the gods had protected him. I take it that this episode, tricked out, imagination winning a solid victory over memory, is rather more than half allegory to show that from early boyhood he was destined to be a poet and a favorite of the gods (Odes III, IV).

Some scholars suggest that Horace's poetic gift may have been due to a strain of Greek blood from southern Italy. One need not, except for fun — scholars are sometimes playful folk — indulge in any such hypothesis. Horace was intensely Latin. Italian sunshine and shade, the myrtle and bay on the slopes of Mount Vultur, the cooing doves, the wild music of the river Aufidus and the blessing of Apollo — you never can tell on what cradle the god will smile — suffice for an explanation.

Another blessing had been granted to the poetic child, his father. Horace the elder was a very unusual man, stuffed with all the traditional virtues of the old Italian stock, and free from its weaknesses. In fact, the whole rural community of Venusia seems to have been robust and full of character. The poet liked to recall his boyhood's memories of the simple, upright life that his neighbors led. The husband, having labored in the fields all day, at sunset homeward wends his weary way, the oxen dragging the ploughshare, and on entering the farm house finds that his wife has penned the goats in the fold, milked them, made a fire on the kitchen hearth, has cooked supper, and brought forth wine, and his day ends with wholesome food, family affection, and untroubled sleep (Epode II). The sons, who digged in the garden, fetched firewood at their mother's bidding, unyoked oxen and did the chores, became good soldiers and helped make the Romans a conquering people (Odes III, VI).

Besides owning a little farm old Horace was a tax-gatherer of some sort, and being economical laid up savings for the education of his darling son. He was a freedman; in what way his ancestors had become slaves nobody knows, it may have been when the Romans first conquered that territory two hundred years before, or perhaps in some suppressed uprising. But Roman slavery does not connote any such social condition as existed in our southern states prior to the Civil War. Often slaves were far better educated than their captors. The more warlike, not the more civilized, nation won battles, and the captives brought to Rome were in things of the mind often far superior to their captors, and slaves frequently performed intellectual as well as manual work in the great Roman households. Private secretaries, librarians, accountants, were often, probably usually, slaves.

Horace's mother is not mentioned, and we may infer that she died in his infancy. His father felt the obligation to play a mother's part. One can fancy the dying wife bidding him do so, as Cornelia, daughter of a Scipio, on her deathbed bade her husband, L. Aemilius Paulus, *Fungere maternis vicibus, pater* (Propertius, Elegies IV, xi). This duty the father most scrupulously performed. According to custom young Horace would have gone to the local school, kept by one Flavius, which was attended by boys of the upper class, sons of old army officers and such, but the father had a higher ambition for his son. Perhaps he recognized his son's exceptional talents, perhaps he was merely carrying out his wife's wishes. At all events, he gave up his business at Venusia, abandoned his farm, and moved to Rome, in order to give his boy the best possible education. By this migration one can measure the father's love for his son. It must have cost the old man a pang to leave the place where he had spent all his life, the stark outline of Mount Vultur against the western sky, the roar of the Aufidus in the wet season and its murmur in the dry, the familiar fields, his place of business, his old cronies. But he did not hesitate.

There is no information as to when they moved to Rome; but if it was time for young Horace to go to a regular boys' school he can hardly have been more than eight or nine years old. We do not know whereabouts in Rome they lived — not on the Palatine where Cicero and other rich and fashionable people dwelt, or near Atticus on the Quirinal, or on the Esquiline, where Maecenas afterwards built a great palace, and Virgil also lived, for that was still waste land, or in that part of the Argiletum where Quintus Cicero bought a house — but there were great numbers of *insulae*, blocks of apartment houses, and we may assume that father and son lived in some simple apartment in a respectable quarter.

The important matter in the father's eyes was not where they lived, but where his son should go to school, since that was what they had gone to Rome for. The school he chose was one to which the patricians sent their sons. The headmaster came from Benevento; his name was Orbilius. He was a man of sternness and vigor; he had been a cavalry officer in his younger days and then had abandoned barracks for the schoolroom, where he maintained military discipline. He did not spare the rod, and he is less known to us from the statue which his admiring fellow townsfolk erected in his honor at Benevento than from Horace's epithet *plagosus*, which Sir Walter Scott would have translated "Cleishbottom."

It seems that Horace senior must have been able to lay by a considerable sum of money, for not only did he accept the greater expenses of Rome — rent, food, school fees — but he dressed his son well and sent him about with attendant slaves. Had you met the boy you would have said that his father must be possessed of inherited wealth (Sat. I, vi).

Young Horace may well have learned to speak Greek at Venusia, for both the Latin and Greek languages were spoken there, and that fact may have increased his interest in Greek literature. At Orbilius' school he studied the Iliad (Epis. II, ii) and the early Latin classics: Ennius, Livius Andronicus (240

B.C.), Plautus, and so on. This study of Latin classics, as is sometimes the case with our schoolboys who study English classics too young, did not cause Horace to love them. His teacher seems to have held up Livius Andronicus as "faultless, beautiful, well-nigh perfect" an opinion that struck Horace in later years as amazing. Of Ennius he liked to remember that before the poet set about composing martial verses, he first drank deep (Epis. I, xix). No doubt he was taught to admire Ennius, but if he ever did so as a boy he changed his attitude after he had become familiar with Virgil's elegance, for he speaks (A.P. 260; Epis. II, 1) of Ennius' ponderous verses, of hasty and careless work, of his ignorance of the poetic art, and pokes fun at him:

> Ennius et sapiens et fortis et alter Homerus,
> ut critici dicunt
>
> Ennius, the wise, the strong, a second Homer,
> as critics say

which reminds one of Chaucer's ironical touch,

> A holy man, as monkës are, or ellës shouldë be.

Horace probably got as good an education at Orbilius' school as could be had in Rome; and his father took just as much care with that more important branch of his education, morals. One may guess that the tenderhearted old man was ever mindful of his wife's precepts and of her womanly wishes. He taught his son to be chaste, a quality not common with Italian youth — but Horace calls it *primus virtutis honos*, "virtue's earliest grace" — and also protected him from any act of shame as well as from scandal (Sat. I, vi). To make sure that his son should not be exposed to chance temptations, and there must have been many in the streets of ancient Rome, old Horace would often accompany him to his teachers (*circum doctores aderat*).

This good father, *pater optimus* (Sat. I, iv), taught him the consequences of good and bad conduct by the examples of people they knew or saw. For a lesson against prodigality: "See young Albius, he is so poor because his father was a spendthrift." Against vice: "Look at Scetanus, don't be like him." Against coveting another man's wife: "See Trebonius, his reputation is bad, he was caught *flagrante delicto*." So, too, when he wished to give his son a positive example, the father would say, "See that upright man, honored by his fellow citizens, do as he does." And, in a general way, he would repeat: "Philosophy can teach you theories, but the best way is to follow the precepts of our forefathers. So long as I am your guardian, I can guide you, and when years shall have brought strength to your body and mind, you will be able to paddle your own canoe."

Horace concludes his reminiscences of his father by saying,

Thanks to his training, I am free from vices that lead to ruin; the lesser faults I have are, I hope, excusable. And perhaps Time will help me, and candid friends, and my own better thoughts, which will say to me: "This is the wiser course, if I act thus my life will be nobler, and my dear friends will be pleased. Those things that So-and-so did are not nice, shall I be fool enough to do the like?" After this fashion I argue with myself, and when I have leisure I scribble a little — this is one of those lesser faults of mine to which I referred.

It is a sweet satisfaction to know that the old man did not give his devotion in vain. Of all Horace's good qualities, his pride in his father is the most attractive. It would have been easy for the son of an Apulian peasant, the grandson of a slave, after he had won a firm footing among the most eminent men in Rome with the doors of fashionable society open to him, a place at court offered to him — it would have been easy to yield to the insidious appeal of snobbery, and at least be silent as to his ancestry. Not so Horace. He says: "Never, so long as I am of sound mind shall I be ashamed of such a father." Nor would he do as others did and say that it was not his fault to be born the son of a freedman: "This is far from my way of thinking; if Fate were to give us the opportunity to live our lives over again, and to choose parents to gratify our vanity, I should refuse patrician birth, and be well content with mine."

One cannot but regret that the old man did not live to enjoy his son's renown.

II

THE POLITICAL BACKGROUND

THE high and palmy days of the Roman Republic, as Horace senior and other contemporaries of Cicero looked back upon them, came to an end with the third Punic War and the destruction of Carthage (146 B.C.). The glittering pageant of Roman history had spread throughout all Italy and over the Mediterranean lands, flaunting the great names of Roman heroes, like banners in the breeze — Camillus, Cincinnatus, Marcellus, Regulus, Paullus, Scipio — till the phrase *Civis Romanus sum* had become the most coveted of decorations. To be sure there had been quarrels between the patricians and the common people, yet these had been but temporary clouds in the blue sky of triumph. After the destruction of Carthage things changed. Conquest and booty brought arrogance and insolence in their train. The rich grew richer, the poor poorer, until the chasm between the proprietary classes and the proletariat threatened to ruin the state. The Gracchi stood like gate posts — so, I take it, Horace senior thought — through which Roman history from its golden past proceeded into a vast battlefield of civil war.

Ambitious patriots or demagogues came forward to champion the rights of the poor, and proud nobles, fighting for privilege and tradition, met them face to face. During the fifty years from the death of the Gracchi to the birth of our poet, the political history of Rome seems one long sequence of bloody struggles for power: massacres succeeded by breathing spaces, and then another leap and clutch at the throat of the opposite party. The great Marius, one of the common people, seven times consul, upheld the plebs. Cinna did the same. Both shed civic blood till, as in a tale told by Robert Louis Stevenson, it ran in the scuppers of the ship of state. Then Sulla, proud patrician, took his turn and hewed and hacked political enemies to pieces.

There was a plenty of other wars too, foreign and domestic. Jugurtha, King of Numidia, was deposed (105 B.C.), the Cimbri and Teutones were exterminated (102–101 B.C.), the revolt of the Italian cities was suppressed (90–89 B.C.), the servile insurrection under Spartacus was crushed (73–71 B.C.).

It sounds as if one were reading the annals of a slaughterhouse. Yet we must remember that the people who suffered in the wholesale civil butcheries were for the most part the rich and privileged, the agitators, the prominent. As Horace says (Odes II, x.):

> saepius ventis agitatur ingens
> pinus et celsae graviore casu
> decidunt turres feriuntque summos
> fulgura montis.

He is right. Those that lift their heads high, lofty trees, towers, mountains, and men, are battered by the tempest and the thunderbolt. Palaces were overthrown but humble citizens, who dwelt in cots and huts, went about their daily business unscathed.

In Venusia, except when an army might pass through the town, life probably had gone on as usual, and at the time old

Flaccus and his son moved to Rome, the political world was comparatively quiet. Three men were conspicuous: Pompey, Crassus, and Caesar. Pompey was a successful soldier, eminently a pillar of society; he was so popular that once when a member of the Cato family at a public meeting, but in private capacity, called him a dictator the speaker was nearly murdered. Crassus, a man of colossal wealth, and Julius Caesar, brilliant, audacious, cynical, magnanimous, and very ambitious, were the other two. These three formed a triumvirate and assumed control of the government (60 B.C.). At this Cicero, a devout believer in republican institutions and the customs of the Fathers, was in despair, *Certi sumus perisse omnia,* "I am sure all is lost," he said; but he had no power to block the Triumvirs on their arrogant way.

A few years later Caesar set Rome beside herself with excitement and pride. He invaded Gaul, forced the Helvetii to obey him, drove Ariovistus and his Germans helter-skelter back over the Rhine, conquered the Belgae, and finally carried his legions across the channel, *beluosus oceanus* (teeming with monsters) *in ultimos orbis Britannos* (Odes I, xxxv) to ferocious islanders, *hospitibus feros* (Odes III, iv). The boys at Orbilius' school must have been boisterous with enthusiasm and hot for news. Young Horace was then eleven years of age. Among older people at first there was much apprehension over this expedition to England, report said that frightful reefs protected the island, and that even if Caesar were successful it was doubtful if the conquest would be profitable, for there was no silver in Britain, in fact nothing worth taking except slaves. Later news brought relief. Cicero wrote to his brother Quintus (summer, 54 B.C.), then on Caesar's staff:

Oh! What a welcome letter you wrote me from Britain! I was fearful of the island's coast. What remains of your enterprise I do not underestimate, but there is more ground for hope than for fear, I am more excited by expectation than by apprehension. And I see that you have extraordinarily good subjects to write about, the geography of the land, all sorts of places and things, manners, customs, peoples, battles, and what a general you have!

But as to the political condition of the state Cicero was very gloomy. He wrote to Atticus: "The State has not only lost the sap, the blood, but also the very look and aspect of the former constitution" (October 54 B.C.), and in desperation he turned for comfort to literature and his country estates. The death of Crassus, defeated and killed by the Parthians (53 B.C.), left Pompey and Caesar rivals and it required no prophetic eye to foresee the future. The senatorial party with Pompey at its head sent Caesar an ultimatum. In answer Caesar led his army across the Rubicon, the little river which divided foreign soil from Roman domain and loyalty from rebellion. "I came," Caesar said, "to deliver the Roman people from a faction that oppressed it."

Cicero, after shilly-shallying, espoused Pompey's side. He wrote that Caesar had in his party "all the criminal and social outcasts and all who deserved to be counted as such, all the insolvent, a goodly number, all the profligates, all the lowest city rabble and almost all the young generation," and to this list he soon could add eleven legions and a host of cavalry. He foresaw the inevitable result. "Pompey," he said "is irresolute, sluggish, incompetent with neither spirit nor plan, neither forces nor activity" (February 8, 49 B.C.). Three weeks later he wrote to Atticus again about Caesar:

Do you appreciate what kind of a man he is to whom the government has fallen, how intelligent, how vigilant, how ready. By Hercules, if he neither murders nor robs, he will be dearly loved by those that now fear him most. I have talked a great deal with farmers and people of the country towns — they care for nothing but their fields, their houses and their pennies (March 2, 49 B.C.)

And once more, three weeks later:

In spite of all this, we live. Rome is still standing, the judges preside in the law courts, the aediles make preparations for the public games, our political friends add up their profits, and I sit still (March 20, 48 B.C.).

Poor Cicero! He retired to his villa at Formiae and no doubt brooded over his own description of the ideal statesman: "As a safe voyage is the aim of the pilot, as health is the aim of the physician, as victory is the aim of the general, so the ideal statesman will aim at happiness for the citizens of the state, to give them material security, abundant wealth, ample glory and untarnished honor. This is the finest of human achievements."

Cicero hated the idea of a king, but he could not but admire Julius Caesar. Old Horace, though he took no part in politics, probably felt in somewhat the same way. The storms of state, the lightning of civil war did not scathe his humble head, and the routine of life went on about him in its customary way. Orbilius kept his school and wielded his rod, as if the republican constitution of Rome still stood. One may guess that the father, though prudent in communicating his thoughts to outsiders, talked freely with his clever son, and discussed what possible way there might be to retain personal independence, and also secure the benefits of order, which now appeared possible only under a single ruler.

Caesar defeated Pompey at Pharsalus (August 48 B.C.), and afterwards Pompey's partisans in Africa and Spain. Soon his power was absolute, as Horace says (Odes II, 1):

> cuncta terrarum subacta
> praeter atrocem animum Catonis,

> All the world subdued
> except the fierce spirit of Cato.

Pompey had been murdered by men hoping to do Caesar a service, and Cato committed suicide. That hero's act impressed Horace deeply, he speaks (Odes I, XII) of Cato's *nobile letum,* "noble death," and this shows where his sympathies lay. Bred on the proud traditions of Roman freedom and a scorn of kings, his enthusiasm, all his youthful ideals, were against Caesar. It was not till long afterwards that his natural Epicurean bent, together with altered circumstances, and the genius of Augustus, made him appreciate the primary value of peace and order.

By 46 B.C. the civil war had ended and peace was once more restored. Horace's father probably had died, and Horace, now nineteen, set out, no doubt in accordance with plans made beforehand, to pursue his further studies at Athens, the home of intellectual interests.

III

PHILIPPI

I T was the fashion for rich young Romans to go to Athens in
pursuit of culture, and at this time there were a number
there: Bibulus, Acidinus, Tullius Montanus, Tullius Mar-
cianus, Messala Corvinus, and young Marcus Tullius Cicero.
These students came from eminent Roman families, and probably lived on a scale quite out of Horace's reach, even if he had
wished to associate with them; besides, his father had taught
him to live *parce frugaliter,* "thriftily and frugally" (Sat. I, IV).
Messala is the only one he seems to have known. Horace was
studious, they may or may not have been. In the life of gilded
youth at Athens, philosophy and literature were more or less
tempered by Chian wine and black-eyed girls, but Horace was a
good student, industrious and interested.

At Venusia Horace learned, at least so I believe, to speak
Greek colloquially. At Orbilius' school he studied the Iliad, and
no doubt other Greek poetry and prose, and in consequence was
well prepared to take up university work at once. He took
courses, as we would say, in poetry and also in philosophy, as he

wished (so he says) to be able to seek the truth and distinguish right from wrong. In philosophy he studied the tenets of the Stoics, as well as those of the Epicureans and the Platonists. But he already felt the lure of poetry, and read the old Greek lyrical poets with diligence: Archilochus, Alcaeus, Sappho, Anacreon. Of Archilochus (seventh century B.C.), born in Paros, who according to tradition invented iambic verse, Horace says: "I was the first to imitate his moods and meters and show forth the iambics of Paros to the Roman world" (Epis. I, XIX), and he defended such imitation by the examples of Alcaeus and Sappho, who likewise had imitated Archilochus. Horace also says that he was the first to make Alcaeus known in Italy. And no doubt he also studied Pindar, Anacreon, Stesichorus, Callimachus, and others. He was so enamored of the beauty and grace of these lyric poets that at the beginning of his poetical endeavors he composed poems in Greek, but his native good sense appeared to him, in a dream, under the guise of Romulus, and firmly forbade him. This foolish fancy must have come upon him — and left him — while still in the shadow of the Acropolis, for he had already begun to write Latin verses before he went back to Italy.

Suddenly, in 44 B.C., this academic world, both for the drinking set and for the studious, was broken in upon by tremendous news. On the Ides of March, in the Senate Chamber, Julius Caesar had been butchered by a band of conspirators, led by his best friend Marcus Brutus.

The news of Caesar's death struck half the Roman world aghast with fear and anger. The other half hailed the murderers as glorious regicides, heroes of liberty, saviors of the Republic. That very day Cicero wrote to his friend Basilius: "My congratulations to you! Likewise for me! My dear Friend, all of me is at your service. Be kind to me, and keep me informed of what you are doing and of what is going on." And a little later to Atticus: "Our heroes accomplished all that they could most gloriously and splendidly." And to Trebonius he wrote: "That famous feast on the Ides of March." No doubt when the news reached Athens, the young Roman patricians, Messala, Cicero junior, and their friends, and Horace, too, cheered and rejoiced. The slogan "Liberty" is powerful with generous youth. There are times when words shoot across the sky like comets, Freedom! The Cross! La Patrie! Democracy! Their fathers had been afraid of Caesar as an absolute ruler and as a leveling radical, and they had inherited their fathers' beliefs.

However, Athens was many days' journey from Rome, and academic life went on as before. Horace studied the meters of Archilochus, and young Cicero continued to bring Professor Cratippus home to dinner. But at Rome politics assumed a portentous shape. The chief dramatis personae were dazed and bewildered, no man dared trust another. Cicero withdrew to the country and worked over *De Senectute*. One thing is clear, the party of the liberators was outjockeyed. Brutus and Cassius fled from Rome. Brutus certainly did not want civil war, neither did most of his party, but the friends of Julius Caesar were bent on revenge. All was confusion.

One day in the autumn word ran through Athens that Brutus had arrived at the Piraeus. The city was in great excitement. He was well known there and the Athenians gave him a royal welcome. To the young Roman students he was their ideal hero. Of patrician birth, descended from that Junius Brutus who had expelled the last king from Rome, a scholar and philosopher, an idealist who had himself, at the cost of dear personal affection, saved Rome from another king, temperate, ascetic, free from self-love, he seemed to them the embodiment of all the old Roman virtues that had made Rome Rome, and enabled it to conquer the world. They were wild with enthusiasm. How could they help it? Plutarch says:

For his virtues, Brutus was esteemed by the people, beloved by his friends, admired by good men. Even his enemies did not hate him. He was a man of singularly gentle nature, of great spirit, unaffected by anger, or covetousness, or pleasure, steadfast and inflexible of purpose in what he deemed right. Everybody believed in the integrity of his intentions.

Not long after Caesar's assassination Cicero spoke of Brutus' *singularis incredibilisque virtus*, and in a letter to his own son-in-law Dolabella, said: "I have always loved Brutus for his great intelligence, his gracious courtesy, his extraordinary uprightness and constancy."

Brutus had hoped against hope that civil war could be avoided. When he and Cassius were on their way to the east, Antony insulted him and accused him of preparing for war. He wrote back:

Do not flatter yourself that you have frightened us. Fear cannot touch us. If other motives were able to turn us towards civil war, your letter would not deter us, for threats have no power over free men. You know well that we hate war, that hardly anything can drag us into it, and you assume a menacing attitude, no doubt, to make people believe that our resolution is the effect of our fears.

Here are our sentiments. We wish to see you live in honor in a free land. We do not wish to be your enemies, but we rate liberty higher than your friendship. Therefore we pray the Gods to inspire you with counsels salutary to the Republic and to yourself. If not, we desire that your own party may hurt you as little as possible, and that Rome may be free and glorious.

At Athens Brutus lodged with a friend and attended the lectures of Professor Cratippus, but he was also making preparations for the inevitable struggle that he saw looming before him. When a republican partisan sailed in with a rich treasure, Brutus gave a great entertainment. All the guests drank to victory and freedom. Young Cicero was surely present, and probably Horace, for both of them — as well as Messala, Bibulus,

Pompeius, Varus, Marcus Valerius, and the sons of Lucullus, Cato, and Hortensius, and probably almost all the Roman students in Athens — had enlisted as soon as they knew that Brutus meant to fight.

Young Cicero, who had had military experience under Pompey, received command of a squadron of horse, and was to distinguish himself. Brutus spoke of him in the most complimentary terms. Horace, who had no training except what he may have received on the Campus Martius as part of the normal education of a Roman gentleman, was appointed a military tribune. Of these there were six to a legion, so that a tribune corresponded roughly to a colonel in our army. Probably there were not enough experienced officers to go round. And in battle the general relied chiefly on the centurions. Horace was a young man of education, and doubtless commended himself to Brutus by his courage, intelligence, and enthusiasm, and yet his appointment did not escape severe criticism from his aristocratic comrades (Sat. I, vi).

The campaign carried Horace up north through Thessaly and Macedonia, bringing him to a sight of various places famous in Greek mythology. To many of these he refers in his poems. The army then crossed into Asia Minor and passed through Clazomenae, on the bay of Smyrna, where Horace wrote a Latin poem, probably the earliest that has come down to us (Sat. I, vii). It is exceedingly dull and hardly to be excused even to a tired soldier on the march. From Clazomenae Brutus proceeded to Sardis to meet Cassius, who had been gathering together supplies and recruits in Asia Minor and Syria. And there took place between the two commanders the immortal scene that Shakespeare has portrayed. One would like to imagine that Horace as well as Lucius and Titinius had stood on guard outside the tent. The two generals, soon reconciled, made their plans, and took their way across the Bosphorus into Macedonia.

Meanwhile, in Italy the leaders of the Caesarian party, Antony, Octavius, and Lepidus, under the pressure of necessity had overcome the manifold differences between them, and, as a triumvirate, laid hold upon the government. They acted with vigor. Enemies within reach they put to death, afterwards confiscating their property; one hundred senators and two thousand equites, including Cicero, his brother Quintus, and Quintus' son were thus executed. Velleius Paterculus says, "No one has had tears enough to weep the misfortunes of this time." They levied contributions, they collected forces, they crossed the Adriatic, and marched into Macedonia towards Philippi.

After some hesitation the opposing armies met. Plutarch tells the story in his admirable naïf way. On the night before the battle Cassius asked Brutus what he meant to do if they were defeated. Brutus answered: "When I was younger, Cassius, and less experienced in affairs, I held a bold philosophy, and I blamed Cato for killing himself, as doing a cowardly irreligious act, trying to evade the divine course of things, not to meet evil bravely, but to run away from it. But now I am of another mind. If Providence decides against us, I shall strive no more but die content. I gave my life to my country on the Ides of March, and since then for her sake I have lived a second life with liberty and honor."

The military opinion of historical writers seems to be that the republican army, for various reasons, should have stayed within its entrenchments and let the enemy attack; but it did not do so. It issued forth and gave battle. Brutus commanded the right wing; the legion in which Horace was an officer must have gone with him. This wing drove headlong the army of Octavius that faced it, and sacked Octavius' tents. But Cassius, on the left, confronting Mark Antony, had the worst of it, and misled by a belief that Brutus had also been defeated, fell on his sword, or, as some say, commanded his freedman Pandarus to cut off his head. So he perished. Brutus led the army back into its entrenchments.

After more days of impatient waiting Brutus marched out again and gave battle. Appian describes the fight (Horace White's translation):

Both sides divined equally that this day and this battle would decide the fate of Rome completely; and so indeed it did. The onset was superb and terrible. They had little need of arrows, stones or javelins, which are customary in war, for they did not resort to the usual manoeuvres and tactics of battles, but coming to close combat with naked swords, they slew and were slain, seeking to break each other's ranks. . . . The slaughter and the groans were terrible. The bodies of the fallen were carried back and others stepped into their places from the reserves. The generals flew hither and thither looking after everything, exciting the men by their ardour, exhorting the toilers to toil on, and relieving those who were exhausted so that there was always fresh courage at the front. Finally Octavius's soldiers . . . pushed back the Republican line as though they were turning round a very heavy machine. Brutus's men were driven back step by step, slowly at first and without loss of courage. Presently their ranks broke and they retreated more rapidly, and then the second and third ranks in the rear retreated with them, all mingled together in disorder, crowded by each other and by the enemy, who pressed upon them without ceasing until it became plainly a flight.

Brutus escaped from the field with a few friends. It was late at night. Someone said, "We cannot stay here, we must flee." "Yes," Brutus answered, "we must flee, but not with our feet." Then with a glad countenance he bade them all farewell. He said that he found infinite satisfaction in that none of his friends had been false to him. As to Fortune, he was only angry with her for his country's sake, and for himself he deemed himself much happier than the victors, for he was leaving a reputation for virtue such as they could never have. He then withdrew and fell upon his sword.

Cato's son, Lucullus' son, and Hortensius' son, all lost their lives in the battle, and many of Brutus' friends committed suicide. Horace escaped, as did Pompeius Varus, Messala, and young Cicero. Long afterwards, in his ode to his old comrade, Pompeius Varus, Horace says: "You and I fought at Philippi, when Valor was struck down and proud warriors bit the ignoble dust. I not nobly (*non bene*) dropped my shield and shared the terrors of the headlong flight. Nimble Mercury picked me up, wrapped me in a thick cloud, and carried me safe through the enemy." (Odes II, VII). *Sauve qui peut!* All ran that could. It is hardly likely that had Horace done a cowardly act he would have celebrated it. The *non bene* is merely a touch of ironical modesty; he did not possess enough mad heroism to imitate Brutus' self-destruction or Cato's *nobile letum*.

Apart from the poetic haze thrown over the episode by nimble Mercury lies a further haze of uncertainty, because Archilochus, Alcaeus, and Anacreon had all suffered similar experiences in running away from battle, at least in verse.

Horace admired Brutus greatly. One could wish that in his ode to Augustus (Odes I, XII),

> Quem virum aut heroa
> . . . sumis celebrare, Clio?

in which he names a number of famous Roman heroes — Romulus, Numa Pompilius, Scaurus, Aemilius Paulus, Fabricius, Curius, Camillus, Marcellus — he had felt it possible to include Brutus. But it would not have been seemly, and by that time Horace was convinced that the murder of Julius Caesar had been a crime, and that Brutus had been wrong. He had learned to appreciate the value of law and order, which secured to the private citizen many a liberty, if not political liberty. One may say, I think, that the three men who most influenced Horace's life were, during his youth his father, in his young manhood Brutus, and in his maturity Maecenas.

After the victory at Philippi the Triumvirs extended an amnesty to those of their opponents who were ready to submit. Horace took advantage of this, and returned to Rome.

IV

MAECENAS

THE Triumvirs, in order to provide for their own soldiers, had confiscated the lands of persons who had sided with Brutus and Cassius, and Horace on his return from Philippi found that his farm at Venusia had been taken. He went to Rome, where, at first, he hoped to support himself by writing poetry. He says, "After Philippi, as I had been deprived of my father's farm, I was down, my wings were cut, and the prick of poverty drove me to writing verses" (Epis. II, ii). His beginnings could hardly have been profitable. He had, however, enough property of some kind, doubtless inherited from his father, to enable him to buy a post in the state treasury, that of *scriba*, a sort of clerk or secretary to the city quaestor. He must have performed his duties acceptably, or he would hardly have been recommended so warmly to Maecenas as he was a year or two later; but his heart was not in his work, and out of office hours he probably continued to write verses.

His earliest compositions were satires. He had, while serving in Brutus' army, already written one, to which I have referred. And, now that he was back in the great metropolis, where folly and vice abounded, it was natural to take folly and vice as objects of castigation, especially as they must have appeared more conspicuous to him after his sojourn in the quiet university town of Athens. The second Satire in Book One, which I take as an instance, begins:

> Ambubaiarum collegia, pharmacopolae,
> mendici, mimae, balatrones, hoc genus omne,
> Guilds of flute girls, quack apothecaries,
> Beggars, actresses, buffoons, all such,

and goes on in a Hogarthian way about prodigals, gluttons, and whore-mongers. To modern taste the satire is insipid, repellant, dull, and resembles the work of a hungry and unsuccessful young poet living in Grub Street.

The importance of his first poetical efforts lies in this, that they brought him into the company of other young poets and men of letters, some of whom were rising into note. Horace was gay, charming, cultivated, and very intelligent, and we soon find him good friends with Virgil and Varius, two young men a little older than himself, both devoted to poetry and both close friends of Maecenas. Virgil, like Horace, had possessed a farm which had been confiscated, and sharing that hard experience must have helped bring the two young men into sympathy. But Virgil had powerful friends, in especial C. Asinius Pollio, statesman, orator, historian, and poet, and Cornelius Gallus, also a soldier, politician, and poet, and they by their intervention finally secured a small landed estate for him in Campania. Pollio also introduced Virgil to Maecenas, who in the absence of Octavius was already the foremost citizen in Rome, both socially and politically.

By this time (39 B.C.) Virgil and Varius were on such a footing with Maecenas that they felt they possessed the right to introduce Horace to him. Horace has left an account of that first meeting (Sat. I, vi). Virgil had broached the subject to Maecenas, telling him of Horace; and Varius supported Virgil's commendation. Thereupon Horace was duly brought into the presence of the statesman, already as I say, eminent, though little if at all older than Horace, both men being about twenty-six. Horace, the freedman's son, felt shy in the presence of one of the most important men in the realm, imagining no doubt that Maecenas was looking on him not merely as the friend of the two poets, but also as an ex-officer in Brutus' army. All Horace could do was to stammer out a few words. He stated what he was — a freedman's son, country born, bred in Rome, educated at Athens — that he had been a tribune in the Republican army, and (I am sure) he spoke bravely of Brutus and the Republican cause. He must have added that he had accepted the amnesty, had found his farm confiscated, and was working on a job in the treasury but wished to be a poet. Maecenas, as was his way, answered but little, and Horace withdrew. For some unknown reason Horace heard nothing for nine months; then Maecenas sent for him, made him welcome, opened his doors to him, and received him into the circle of his particular friends (38 B.C.). Horace says he deemed it a great honor to have found favor in Maecenas' eyes. Maecenas' friendship was of prime consequence in Horace's life, and endured till death parted them.

Gaius Cilnius Maecenas was a very remarkable man. He lives in history together with M. Vipsanius Agrippa, as one of the two men, by whose wisdom, energy, and loyalty Octavius was able to convert a dying chaotic Republic into a living, ordered Empire. He was of royal birth. Every school boy knows the first line in the first book of Odes,

Maecenas atavis edite regibus

Maecenas was descended from the ancient kings of Etruria, and was proud of his lineage, yet not so much so but that Horace, after their intimacy had been well established, ventured to twit him a little on his royal descent, at least it seems so to me. My reasons for believing that Horace indulged himself in a little ironical raillery are these: for years Horace's mode of address had been *Amice Maecenas*! *Care Maecenas, Jocose Maecenas, Beate Maecenas, Candide Maecenas, Dilecte Maecenas*, and now when giving an invitation to a simple meal beneath a poor man's roof, flanked by a mellowing jar, in an ode which ends with a eulogy on the man who cares not for the gifts of Fortune or the accident of birth, but is content to be poor and honest, he apostrophizes Maecenas magniloquently, as *Tyrrhena regum progenies* (Odes III, xxix). Horace was a republican at heart, and he knew that Maecenas knew it. Hence the little pleasantry.

If it was a weakness in Maecenas to be proud of his royal descent, it was not very serious, I think. He labored all his life for his country and his emperor, and sought nothing for himself; he was devoted to his friends, and in return only asked for affection. He was modest and simple. He built, it is true, a great palace on the Esquiline hill — which before had been a neglected spot, where paupers were buried, rubbish was dumped, and old hags acquired a reputation for witchcraft — but this he did in accordance, as I believe, with Augustus' wish to embellish the city. Here he entertained the wit and fashion of Rome. He was a most unselfish and wise adviser to his master, and deserved well of him. The historian Dio assigns to him a long speech at the time when Octavius was deciding upon the form the state should take, whether republican or monarchical, which in substance might have been made by Alexander Hamilton, or Queen Elizabeth's Lord Burleigh, so full of good sense it was, so broad in view. He was interested in literature, sought the society of men of letters, wrote himself various compositions, tragedies, a treatise on precious stones, a history of animals, and so on. All these have been lost, and historians have assumed that the loss is not greatly to be regretted, but this variety of interest shows a roving and inquisitive mind. His diction was sometimes highfalutin; commentators lay stress on some chance humorous chaff by Augustus, who twitted Maecenas upon his "myrrh-scented" verses. To me such a criticism merely suggests that both men were young and very intimate. Augustus composed literary works himself, and it was most natural that he should make fun of his friend's poetry.

Maecenas, also, was of cultivated taste in the fine arts. In Greek sculpture he admired Lysippus, Phidias, and Praxiteles; in Greek painting, Apelles and Parrhasius; and among the early Greek silversmiths, Mintor and Mys, artists famous in their time (Propertius, Elegies III, ix).

There are stories, reported by Seneca, Juvenal, Suetonius, men of later generations who got their gossip by hearsay, that he was careless in dress, florid in language, fond of wine, liked to listen to rippling waters, and beguiled his leisure with a thousand whimsies. To me these occupations appear not inappropriate to the leisure of an intellectual statesman in intervals between strenuous labors. Nevertheless, imagine my astonishment to read in John Buchan's admirable book on Augustus, "He [Maecenas] had all the foibles of the aesthete and the foppishness of the *petit-maître*." This strikes me as a judgment not less extraordinary than erroneous. Maecenas was fastidious, he was modest, he was self-effacing, and he conducted most grave and important business with consummate skill. Do you think Augustus would have sent a *petit-maître* as envoy to Mark Antony, that rude, roaring, drinking, magnificently masculine, swashbuckler of a soldier, Cleopatra's "man of men"?

Years afterward, when Maecenas was at the peak of his power

and reputation, Propertius says to him in an elegy: "You shrink from all publicity. Though as magistrate you may plant your lictors' axes where you wish, and issue decrees in the Forum, though Augustus gives you all necessary resources, though riches pour in, you draw back in lowly guise into obscurity" (Elegies III, ix). Is that like a *petit-maître*? As to his dress: Buchan calls him a fop and Seneca accuses him of slovenliness. Both consider him effeminate. But whether he was overfond of haberdashery, or negligent, I take it that Maecenas dressed for comfort and to please himself, indifferent to the sartorial code of the Palatine Hill; very likely he adhered to provincial habits learned in Etruria, where his ancestors had been kings and accustomed to set the fashion, not to follow it.

It is easy to see how other unfavorable criticism arose. Some men, such as Horace describes in "The Bore," who tried to push their way into Maecenas' house and make his acquaintance against his will, met with a smart rebuff, and in their vexation called him a snob, a fop, a scented littérateur and what not.

It is also easy to understand how the military mind was affected. Velleius Paterculus (30 A.D. ?), an old soldier, describes him as "a man who while displaying sleepless vigilance, foresight and capacity for action in all critical emergencies, yet during the intervals of relaxation was in his indolent self-indulgence almost more effeminate than a woman." We all know how Harry Hotspur was affected on the battlefield by the young swell "neat and trimly dressed, perfumed like a milliner," and how the gait of mincing poetry set his teeth on edge, and it may well be that many old Roman soldiers, used to blood and mud and sweat, to fighting on beaches, hills and woods and city streets, were completely disgusted when they heard stories of how Maecenas and Horace, their hair anointed with nard, their heads with roses crowned, sat under an elm tree, drank Caecuban, exchanged verses and listened to Lydia play on her ivory lyre. But, one may ask, what would they have said, if he, a grave statesman, had written detective stories?

As for Seneca's strictures, he was a self-conscious stoic, and could hardly be sympathetic with Epicurean enjoyment of life. He took special offense at Maecenas' saying that he loved life so dearly that, rather than die, he would choose to live in any torments. But what most troubled Seneca was Maecenas' literary style, turgid, bombastic, guilty of all sorts of rhetorical faults, at least in Seneca's opinion; and he, anticipating Buffon's aphorism, asserted, but in reverse of cause and effect, *le style, c'est l'homme*, "He would have been a man of great powers . . . had he not been so loose in his style of speech."

But the decisive answer to Buchan's contemptuous appellatives lies in the affection and admiration which Virgil, Augustus, and Horace felt for Maecenas; Horace who was the last man in the world to put up with a fop and a *petit-maître*, and Augustus, who manifested the greatest trust in Maecenas' foresight, wisdom, capacity for diplomacy and administration, qualities rarely if ever found in a fop or *petit-maître*. Horace calls Maecenas *Decus Equitum*, Virgil apostrophizes him, *O Decus, o famae merito pars maxima nostrae, Maecenas*, "O ornament of glory, O thou to whom the best part of my fame is due"; and Propertius said that if he were to write of heroes, he would not sing the deeds of the Titans, nor of Homer's warriors, nor of Xerxes giving commands to the sea, nor the founding of Rome, nor the destruction of Carthage, nor of Marius's victories, but he would recount the deeds of Augustus Caesar and next after that the deeds of Maecenas. Propertius also calls him *Maecenas, nostrae spes invidiosa juventae*, "Maecenas, hope and envy of our Roman youth." Could or would these poets use such language of Maecenas, if he had been a fop and a *petit-maître*?

To this defense of Maecenas I may add that he was very popular with the citizens of Rome. When, after an illness, he appeared at the theatre, there was such a tumultuous shout of applause that Tiber's banks and the Vatican Hill echoed and reëchoed again and again (Odes I, xx; II, xvii).

At this period of their lives Maecenas and Horace were both young men, both believed in enjoying life, both thought well of good food, of good wine, of poetry and friendship, and of pretty girls skillful in song or with the lyre. Like Horace, Maecenas was ready to lay serious affairs aside and *desipere in loco.* The poet dedicated each of his four volumes, or at least the first book in each volume, Odes, Epodes, Satires, and Epistles, to Maecenas. A number of these poems show a most affectionate familiarity. I will quote from two of them.

One tells how Maecenas had played a gastronomic jest on Horace, by bidding his cook put a great deal of garlic in some dish, to Horace's nauseous disgust. The poet cries out, "O facetious Maecenas, if you ever play me such a trick again, I pray that your girl will put up her hands to ward off your kisses" (Epode III).

The other (Odes II, xii) celebrates Terentia (whose name is veiled by the cognomen of Licymnia), a beautiful young lady, whom Maecenas recently as it seems, had married, a sister of that Licinius Murena who was afterwards accused of plotting against Augustus and put to death.

Me the Muse bids acclaim the sweet singing of Mistress Licymnia,
How brightly her eyes flash, how true her heart in your mutual love,

She that so gracefully danced with the dancers,
Jested with jesters, and in the worship to Diana consecrate,
Tossed her white arms in the air with the maidens.

Would you, Maecenas, barter a lock of her tresses
For all the heaped wealth of the monarchs of Persia,
Or, for the riches of fruitfullest Phrygia,
Or the full palaces of the Arabians,

When she turns you her throat for your passionate kisses,
Or, cruelly coquettish, refuses to take them,
Although she delights even more than the asker
To have them snatched from her, or steals them herself?

Maecenas always, in spite of disputes, dearly loved his wife.
Long years afterwards slander busied itself with her and the
Emperor Augustus. This story I do not believe. Buchan says
it is improbable. Augustus was trying hard to raise the moral
tone of Roman society and condemned adultery; he loved his
own wife, Livia; Maecenas was his loyal friend; and the charge
of sexual misbehavior was, as always, a handy insult in the
hands of a disappointed politician. An aggrieved parasite who
began by calling the man who snubbed him a snob, would cheer-
ily go on to call him a cuckold, or anything else.

I repeat, Virgil's and Horace's affection and respect for Maecenas give the lie to all those detractions that started who knows
where, and first found utterance after he had been dead for
thirty, sixty, a hundred years. One may rest assured that Maecenas was a true gentleman, of fine manners and generous sympathies, of quick intelligence and great tact, a genuine patriot
who wished to benefit his country materially, intellectually, and
morally. He was Horace's dearest friend, and when he came to
die wrote to Augustus, *Horati Flacci, ut mei, esto memor,* "Be as
mindful of Horace as you would of me."

V

THE TRIP TO BRINDISI

THE political sky was dark. To the farsighted, and also to those who were not, it was obvious after this victory at Philippi that two stars could not take their courses in one sphere, that the Roman world was too small for both Octavius and Antony, do what they would to preserve amity. Both men wished to avoid a catastrophe, and with this in view Octavius sent an embassy to Antony. Maecenas was one of the envoys, and to make the journey pleasant, and also perhaps to throw a cloak over the seriousness of the expedition and give it the aspect of a party of pleasure, Maecenas invited several friends to accompany him as far as Brindisi. This was in the summer of 38 B.C., or perhaps 37 B.C. Horace tells the story in one of his narrative poems (Sat. I, v). The journey began at Rome and took its course via the Appian Way.

I left the great city of Rome, and put up at Aricia in a simple inn. My companion was Heliodorus, the rhetorician, by far the most learned of the Greeks. Our next stop was Forum Appi, crowded with boatmen and rascally tavern-keepers. We were lazy and took this stretch [about 40 miles] in two sections, though fast travellers do it in a single day. The Appian Way is pleasanter if you take it slowly. Here, on account of the water which is foul, I ate nothing, and waited impatiently while my companions had their dinner. [At this town they took passage on the canal boat.]

By this time night was beginning to let her shades fall upon the earth and to scatter stars throughout the sky. The porters bawled at the boatmen, and the boatmen bawled back at the porters: "Dock here!" "You're putting in three hundred!" "Hi! That's enough." It took a whole hour to collect the fares and harness the mule. What with vicious gnats and marsh-frogs it was impossible to sleep, especially as the drunken boatman sang of the girl he left behind him, and a passenger caught up the song. At long last the passenger got tired and went to sleep, and the lazy boatman tied the reins of his mule to a stone post, turned the beast out to graze, lay down and snored. When day broke we discovered that the canal boat was not moving. A hotheaded passenger jumped out, picked up a willow cudgel, and belabored both mule and boatman over head and body.

It was ten o'clock by the time we finally landed. We washed our hands and faces in the river Feronia. We then had breakfast and crept on three miles and uphill to Anxur [Tarracina], which you see from far away perched on her shining white rocks. At this place Maecenas and Cocceius best of men, envoys sent on business of great weight, and both well used to reconcile quarrelling friends, were to meet us. As my eyes were sore I anointed them with black ointment, and while I was engaged in doing this, Maecenas and Cocceius arrived and with them Fonteius Capito, a most finished gentleman, one of Mark Antony's best friends.

We were thankful to leave the town of Fundi and its "praetor," Aufidius Luscus, and amused by that silly official's ostentation, his bordered toga, broad stripe, and pan of charcoal. Next we stayed in the city of the Mamurra family, where Murena [Maecenas' brother-in-law] lent us his villa, and Capito furnished the supper. The next day dawned most delightfully welcome, for Plotius, Varius [they became Virgil's literary executors], and Virgil joined us at Sinuessa; the earth never bore souls more spotless white than theirs, nor can any one else be so dear a friend to me. How we exulted and hugged one another. So long as I am of sound mind, I shall never rate anything so high as the company of a delightful friend.

A little house next to the Campanian bridge offered us a roof, and the turnpike officials, as is required of them, provided us with wood and salt. Leaving there we arrived at Capua in good season and the mules were relieved of their pack saddles. Maecenas set off to play ball, but Virgil and I went for a nap, as playing ball does not suit the sore-eyed and the dyspeptic. From Capua we journeyed on to Cocceius' luxurious villa, which lies beyond the inns of Caudium. [I omit the account of buffooneries of two yokels provided for their amusement, for though Horace says, "We sat late at supper in high good humour," the episode is boring to modern ears.]

From this place we proceeded direct to Beneventum where our bustling host almost set the house on fire. While he was roasting skinny thrushes on the spit, a burning brand fell out and fire spread through the whole kitchen, flames flared up and licked the roof. Then you should have seen the hungry guests and the frightened servants rescue the food, and all exert themselves to put out the fire.

After we left there Apulia began to show her hills, so familiar to me, hot from the sirocco, and we would never have succeeded in creeping over them had we not stopped at a villa near Trivicum. Here smoke brought tears to our eyes for they had put fresh leaves and green wood on the fire. . . .

From that halting place we drove rapidly twenty-four miles to spend the night in a little town, the name of which will not fit into verse, but easy to indicate, for here that least costly of commodities, water, is bought and sold. But the bread is so delicious that a sensible traveller carries away a load of it on his shoulders, for at Canusium (a town founded long ago by brave Diomede) the bread is full of sand, and there is not a jugful more water. At this town Varius left us much to the grief of his sorrowing friends.

From there we went to Rubi, tired out, for the road we took was long and badly washed by the rains. The next day the weather was better, but the road was worse, all the way to the fishing town of Bari. We had a jolly good laugh at Gnatia, a town built under the displeasure of the water nymphs [i.e. waterless] for an effort was made to persuade us that without fire frankincense would melt on an altar at the threshold of the temple. Apella, the Jew, may believe it, I shan't. For I have learned from Lucretius that "the Gods lead a life free from care," and that if Nature displays something that seems miraculous, it does not mean that the Gods were angry and dropped it down from the high halls of heaven. Well, Brindisi marks the end of a long journey and of a long story.

It had been a long journey, some three hundred and sixty miles, and had taken fifteen days. Horace presumably went back to Rome, while Maecenas and the other envoys continued their journey to meet Antony's representatives.

VI

LIFE IN ROME

ROME, during these dubious years between the Battle of Philippi (42 B.C.) and that of Actium (31 B.C.), lived in peace but never quite free from apprehension. At times danger seemed to come near. In Umbria there had been a revolt of dispossessed landowners, fostered by Antony's wife Fulvia and his brother Lucius, but that had been suppressed (40 B.C.); Sextus Pompey, son of Pompey the Great, had frightened the Italian coasts with his piratical fleet, but he too had been defeated (36 B.C.). Antony was in the East, fighting Parthia or pleasure-seeking at the feet of Cleopatra. Rome half hoped, half pretended to hope, that the agreement between the two conquerors, by which Antony had taken the East and Octavius the West, would hold and prevent civil war. In the city itself life went its routine way, business was transacted as usual in the Forum, and the men of letters worked at verse and prose. Virgil occupied himself with the Georgics, and Varro with a

book on agriculture. Of the general routine Horace gives us an
ironical glimpse in the following story (Sat. I, ix):

I happened to be walking down the Via Sacra meditating, as my custom
is, on some trifling matter, and was wholly absorbed in my thoughts, when
a fellow whom I knew only by name, ran up, seized my hand, crying,
"How do you do, my dear, dear Boy?" "Nicely as things go," I answered,
"and I hope that all goes well with you."

As he kept close beside me, I put in, "Is there anything you want?" He
replied, "You know that I am a man of letters." So I said, "I esteem you
the more for that."

I was on pins and needles, and tried to get away from him. Sometimes
I walked faster, sometimes I would stop and whisper to my servant, while
sweat trickled down to my ankles. "O Bolanus!" * I kept saying to myself, "how blessed it would be to have your temper," while the fellow kept
on chattering about God knows what and praising the various districts of
the city.

As I did not answer, he said, "You are dreadfully anxious to get away.
I have noticed this for some time, but you won't succeed. I shall stick to
you. I will accompany you wherever you go."

To this I replied, "There is no need of you being lugged around. I am
going to visit a man you don't know. He is ill in bed, far away, across the
Tiber near Caesar's gardens."

"Oh, I've nothing to do, and I'm not lazy. I'll go with you all the way."

I dropped my ears like a cross donkey when too heavy a load is laid on
his back. Then he began: "If I am not much mistaken, you will like me
quite as much as you do Viscus or Varius. Who can write more verses than
I, or quicker? Who can limber his legs and dance more lightly? And I
sing so that Hermogenes † might envy me."

Here was my chance to get a word in. I asked, "Have you got a mother,
any relations, who are dependent on your good health?"

"Not one, I have buried them all." (I thought to myself) "O lucky
creatures! But I survive! Oh, finish me! That tragic fate, predicted for

* A hothead.
† A professional singer.

me when I was a boy by a Sabine fortuneteller, as she shook her magic urn, draws nigh:

'Him, that neither poison dire,
Nor hostile sword shall carry off,
Nor pleurisy, nor gout, nor fatal cough —
A chatterbox shall consume like fire:
If, growing up, he be sagacious
He will steer clear of the loquacious.' "

We had come to the Temple of Vesta, the time was past nine o'clock, and it happened that he was bound to attend court and file an answer to a complaint, under penalty of losing his case.

"As you are my friend," he said, "please come to my help, only a little while."

"On my life, I can't be of use, I don't know anything about law, and I am in a hurry to make my visit, as you know."

"I don't know what to do," he said, "to abandon you or abandon my suit."

"Oh, abandon me."

"No, I won't do that," he answered, and began to walk on. And I, for it is hard to contend with a victor, followed him.

"How do you stand with Maecenas?" he began again. "There's a man of few friends and a very good mind. No one has ever made better use of his opportunities. If you would present yours truly, you would have a strong supporter, who could render your affairs prosperous. May I die, if you would not push everybody out of your way."

[Horace] "Our relations with Maecenas are not at all what you think. There is no house freer from cabals than his, none more foreign to such behaviour as you suggest. I tell you, it never hurts me that another man is richer or more of a scholar than I. In that house every man stands on his own feet."

[Bore] "You are telling me a strange tale. I can hardly believe it."

[Horace] "Nevertheless, it is so."

[Bore] "You make me all the more eager to get to know him well."

[Horace] "You need nothing more than your desire. With your

merits you are certain to get there. He is a man that can be won, and for that reason he makes approach to him difficult at the beginning."

[Bore] "I shall not fail myself. I will bribe his servants with gifts. And if I am not admitted the first time, I shall not give up. I'll find some opportunity. I'll meet him in the street. I will escort him home. — 'Life grants nought to mortals without much toil.' "

While he was going on in this way, who should come up but Aristius Fuscus, a dear friend of mine, who knew this other man very well. We all stopped. "Where do you come from? Where are you going?" was asked and answered. I quietly took hold of Fuscus' arm and squeezed it — it felt numb — nodded my head and rolled my eyes as signs for him to come to my rescue. The mean fellow with a laugh pretended not to understand me. I grew angry: [to Fuscus] "You were saying, as I remember well, that you had something private you wished to talk to me about."

[Fuscus] "I haven't forgotten, but I will tell you at a more favorable time. Today is the thirtieth Sabbath. Do you want to hurt the feelings of the circumcised Jews?"

"Their rites," I said, "are nothing to me."

[Fuscus] "But they mean something to me. I am not as strong-minded as you. I am an ordinary man. Please excuse me, I will tell you some other time."

Who would believe so black a day could dawn for me! The rapscallion ran away and left me in the lurch.

By great luck the plaintiff in the suit came up, and shouted out [to the Bore], "Where are you off to, you rascal?" and to me, "Will you be a witness for me?" I agreed at once. He hurried the man into court, where there was a great crowd and tremendous noise.

In this way Apollo rescued me.

The episode sounds far from war's alarms, and also far from official duties and the desk of a *scriba*; but perhaps it was a holiday, or perhaps Horace was already in possession of his Sabine farm and had given up his position in the treasury.

There is another passage (Sat. I, VI) that describes the poet's life in Rome, and his contentment with it.

I go out alone and stroll where my fancy leads. I stop at shops and ask the price of flour and of green vegetables. At the end of the afternoon I wander about the Circus, among the cheats there, or often in the Forum. I listen to the fortunetellers. Then I go home to my dinner of leeks and peas and pancakes. I have three servants to wait upon me at table. On the sideboard, with its marble top, stand two goblets and a ladle, together with a cheap saltcellar, a jug, and a libation bowl of Campanian ware. After that I go to sleep undisturbed by any thought that I must get up early in the morning, walk past the statue of Marsyas (the expression of whose face says he can't bear to look at the usurers there) and go on to the Forum. I lie abed till ten. Then I take a stroll, or, after having read or written something that may please me when I think it over, I anoint myself with oil [preparation for exercise]. . . . Then when I am tired, or the hot sun bids me go to the baths, I leave the Campus and the game of ball. I take a light lunch, enough to keep me from going the whole day on an empty stomach, and I while away the time at home.

This is the kind of life that men lead, who are free from the pains and burdens of ambition. And in this way I comfort myself with the thought that I shall live happier than if my father, my uncle, and my grandfather had been quaestors.

At the time he wrote this, it seems as if he must have given up his clerkship in the treasury.

VII

THE SATIRES, BOOK I

HORACE published his first book of Satires in 35 B.C. It consists of ten poems in hexameter verse, that range in length from thirty-five to one hundred and forty three lines. We call them satires; Horace himself calls them sometimes *satirae* and sometimes *sermones*. In fact some are satires in our sense of the word, and others are as he says *sermones*, talks, causeries; bits of discourse on various subjects. The word *satirae* itself meant a mixture, a hotchpotch, a medley.

The Romans were proud of this form of verse, for it was the only one that they had invented; all the others, ode, elegy, epistle, pastoral, epic, drama, they had adapted from the Greek. If you are curious concerning the origin of the satire, scholars will guide you back to Ennius, Pacuvius, Livius Andronicus, but for us it is sufficient to mention Lucilius, who, Horace says, was the true inventor of the literary satire. Lucilius was a man of distinction, uncle to Pompey the Great, very rich, and a member of the illustrious set of Scipio Africanus, the younger, Laelius, and Terence. He wrote thirty books of *Satirae*, of which many fragments are preserved, over 1300 verses. Horace had studied him diligently. All this lies below the horizon of those who read Horace merely for pleasure, and therefore does not concern me. I shall content myself with running through Horace's Satires (Book I); literary compositions that hardly deserve to be called poems — Horace himself says of them, "You would not count anyone a poet who writes as I do, lines more akin to prose" (Sat. I, iv) — and I shall make such comments as may help the reader decide whether he wants to read them himself.

The book is dedicated to Maecenas, and the first satire begins in a friendly colloquial manner:

How does it happen, Maecenas, that no man is contented with his lot, whether he has received it by chance, or adopted it by choice, but envies men who pursue a different vocation? The soldier exclaims, "O lucky merchant!" The sailor cries, "O fortunate soldier!" . . . The lawyer wishes he were a farmer, . . . and yet if a god offered to change their lives, they would refuse.

And all these men say they labor and risk danger to lay by enough wealth for old age, nevertheless they never stop so long as they see another man richer than themselves. What good does it do them? . . . no man can eat but so much. . . . They all want the more that they cannot reach. . . . . They are like Tantalus, and mark: change names and the moral points its finger at you, *mutato nomine de te fabula narratur*. Riches make you fear to lose them, and miserliness makes everybody dislike you. *Est modus in rebus* — there is measure in all things.

. . . Why does a man always compare himself with the few richer . . . instead of with the far greater number of the poorer? . . . So the world goes. It is very rare that we find a man who when his days are counted will say, I have had a happy life and leave it contentedly like a guest who has eaten his fill,

> Inde fit ut raro, qui se vixisse beatum
> dicat et exacto contentus tempore vita
> cedat uti conviva satur, reperire queamus.

There, you have a specimen of Horace's ironical contemplation of life, of his good temper and his good sense, and there, too, are several of those happy phrases — I shall quote others as I proceed — which have passed into general use and show that he was one of the master craftsmen of language.

Satire II begins as I have quoted in an earlier chapter, *Ambubaiarum collegia, pharmacopolae*, and goes on in a dull coarse strain, such as one may find in eighteenth-century English satire. I am told that the poem is based "upon the erotic literature of the Hellenistic period," and Professor Fairclough calls it an "immature and forbidding sketch, coarse and sensational in tone." Let us leave it at that and push on. I will only remark that the phrase — Horace can never help being quotable — *laudatur ab his, culpatur ab illis*, was taken by the quick-witted Beaumarchais, turned into *loué par ceux-ci, blamé par ceux-là* and now stands, or in happier days used to stand, at the head of the Parisian newspaper, *Le Figaro*.

Satire III begins pleasantly enough: "All singers have their faults; if in a company of friends they are asked to sing, they always raise some objection, if they are not asked, they never stop." Such contemporary allusions as the verses may contain have been completely lost; and there is nothing of present interest in the satire except three lines which show how intimate Horace had become with Maecenas: "If a simple-minded man (such as I have shown myself to you, Maecenas) interrupts you with his chatter while you are reading, or when you wish to be let alone, we say that he lacks *savoir vivre*."

Number IV deals with satire and literary criticism. There, too, is an immortal phrase: *os magna sonaturum*. I have already quoted the one interesting passage in the poem, when he tells how his father instructed him in virtue by pointing out men ruined by their vices, or honored for their virtues.

Satire V is the Trip to Brindisi.

Satire VI is dedicated to Maecenas, and begins with a fine compliment:

> Non quia, Maecenas, Lydorum quidquid Etruscos
> incoluit finis, nemo generosior est te,
> nec quod avus tibi maternus fuit atque paternus,
> olim qui magnis legionibus imperitarent,
> ut plerique solent, naso suspendis adunco
> ignotos, ut me libertino patre natum.

> Though of all Lydians who inhabit Tuscany, none are
> Of nobler birth than you, and though your ancestors
> Both on your mother's and your father's side,
> Commanded great legions, long ago, yet you,
> Maecenas, do not as most men do, turn up your nose
> At unknown men, like myself, a freedman's son.

And the poet goes on to tell of his introduction to Maecenas, and to describe his life in Rome, some of which I have already quoted.

Satire VIII is one of several compositions that deal with witches, and seem to me coarse, dull, and eminently skippable. To picture a witch you have to be a Shakespeare and put into her cauldron "liver of blaspheming Jew" and other similiar ingredients, or a Coleridge, and rouse the reader's tenderness for the lovely lady Christabel. Canidia, Horace's witch, is merely repulsive. His kind heart and his good sense were insurmountable obstacles to his success in this genre.

Satire IX recounts the tale of the bore.

Number x contains a discussion of satire, of Lucilius, and of contemporary poetry and analogous matters. It is interesting only to the scholar, except for its references to Horace's particular friends. Fundanius writes charming comedies; Pollio tells stories of dead kings in iambic trimeter; Varius, without a rival shapes the heroic epic; and Virgil had received from the country-loving Muses smoothness and grace, *molle atque facetum*, which others have variously rendered as "tenderness and grace," "simplicity and charm," and "smoothness and exquisite finish." And he enumerates the men whose approval he covets, Plotius and Varius (who were to be Virgil's literary executors), Maecenas, Virgil, and Valgius (a poet to whom he was to write Odes II, ix), Octavius, another poet, Aristius Fuscus (who failed him in the encounter with the bore, and to whom he addressed the Ode, *Integer Vitae*), the brothers Viscus, Asinius Pollio, Messala Corvinus his old friend and an adherent of Brutus, and Messala's brother, Gellius Publicola who was consul in 36 B.C., Bibulus, a stepson of Marcus Brutus, and Furnius, consul in 17 B.C.: "In their eyes I should like these verses, such as they are, to find favor."

These men whom he enumerates constitute *la crême de la crême* of Roman society. Several are very close in fame to Maecenas and Agrippa. Varius wrote a tragedy, *Thyestes*, perhaps the best tragedy in Latin literature. Asinius Pollio was "the first critic of the period, and a magnificent patron of art and science" (Mackail). He wrote tragedy, and a *History of the Civil Wars*, and distinguished himself in civil and military life. Messala was perhaps the most eminent of all. A contemporary panegyric has come down to us, by an unknown author:

Messala, I will sing of thee though your celebrated worth frightens me. My weak capacities may not bear the strain, yet I will begin, and if my verses fall short of your due praise, for I am a poor chronicler of deeds so great . . . it is enough for me to have shown my willingness . . . and may this humble effort be welcome, and may I be able to compose more and more verses in your honor. . . . You have the advantage of ancient race, but you are not content with the renown of your ancestors . . . you strive to surpass those old honors, and bestow greater luster on your posterity than your ancestry has bestowed on you. . . . Who does greater things than you whether in the field or in the law courts?

VIII

THE SABINE FARM

With the publication of his first book of Satires (35 B.C.), Horace had definitely arrived. His friends were the intellectual and social elite of Rome, and these friends must have often said to one another: What a shame it is that a poet of such possibilities should have to spend his time working over figures, accounts, and reports in the treasury — Pegasus hitched to the plow — he surely should be set free to live in the country which he loves, where far from the noise and turmoil of Rome he may compose poems to his heart's content.

Perhaps Maecenas acted without prompting. He may have waited, as Horace was a proud and independent Roman, until their friendship was so intimate and complete that it had reached the rare point where gifts could be given without ruffling of self-respect and even without arousing surprise. At all events, in the year 33 B.C., when Horace was thirty-two years old, Maecenas presented him with the celebrated Sabine farm, and crowned his life with golden content. Few men have been able to do so much for a friend.

The farm lay some twenty-eight miles to the northeast of
Rome. To reach it a visitor left the city by the Via Valeria. On
reaching Tibur (Tivoli) he continued on the right bank of the
Anio (Aniene) some seven miles to the town of Varia (Vico
Varo). A mile further on he took the road to the left that runs
alongside the little river Digentia (Licenza), a tributary of the
Anio, and continued some four miles. Here, on a knoll to the
left above the stream, is the site of Horace's house. At least so
it seems to me, for the landscape suits this identification. On the
knoll I have mentioned visitors stare at bits of foundations of a
house, at outlines of a walled garden, ninety feet long, and they
are shown vestiges of a terrace, of an atrium, and of three rooms
adorned with black and white mosaics. Scholars have had a delightful time for some two hundred years disputing the site of
the house, but for the time being, archaeologists appear to be in
a happy state of certainty.

These scholars have a similar pleasure — still have, I might
say, for I do not know of a court that can render a final judgment — in debating the site of the *Fons Bandusiae*. It is wise in
these matters to accept the opinion of those most confident in
their own. There is, up the mountain path, far enough from the
house to make an expedition something of a circumstance and
yet not too far, a spring of flashing water darting forth from a
rocky cave under the foliage of an ilex tree, protected by the
shade of Mons Lucretilis — and Professor Tenney Frank is
ready, I infer, to follow Mr. Grimwig's example and "eat his
head" if that is not the place.

It was a lovely spot. The deep-shadowing mountains behind,
the friendly Digentia in front, glades, woods, fields, oaks, pines,
vineyards, cattle, sheep, goats, a comfortable house, a cellar with
Falernian — and at times costlier wines — what more could a
poet, a confirmed bachelor ask? The farm, which seems to have

consisted in part of upland fields on the mountain slopes, was large. Horace could lease portions of it to five tenants, and yet keep for himself a home farm, on which he employed eight slaves. He was delighted with the gift. It meant not merely freedom from drudgery, but all the joys of country life: walking about his own fields, inquiring of his bailiff about his own crops, and watching his own goats; perhaps it meant sitting in front of his own house under a pine tree, and there, master of all he surveyed, brooding over iambics, trochees, dactyls, rereading Alcaeus and Sappho, and waiting for friends to come out of town to dinner. He expressed his feelings toward his acquisition in the famous satire (Sat. II, vi) beginning *Hoc erat in votis*:

This is what I have been praying for. A plot of land not very large, with a garden and a spring that never dries up near the house, and beyond these woodland! But the Gods have done more and better than this for me. It is indeed well with me. O Mercury, I ask for nothing more except that you confirm these gifts as my very own, never to be taken from me.

If I have not increased my property by guile,
If I shall not diminish it by vice or fault,
If I do not become a fool and utter prayers like these:
O that that disfiguring tongue of land that juts
into my farm could be incorporate in it!
O that Luck would uncover a treasure trove! . . .
If I am content and grateful for what I have, I make
this prayer to Thee:
O make my flocks fat and all else that I possess,
except my wits, and please continue to be my best
guardian!
Now that I have left Rome for my castle in the hills,
what should I praise in the Satires of my prosaic Muse,
sooner than my farm?

He loved the place all his life. In his epistle (Epis. I, xvi) to his friend Quinctius he says:

Dear Quinctius, to anticipate your asking
Whether my farm's arable land supports
Its master, or whether it is his olives
And orchards that make him rich,
Or its meadows, and vine-covered elms?
I will be loquacious and write you about
The nature and lie of the land.
        There is a line of hills, unbroken
Except by one dark valley, which runs south in such a way that
The rising sun looks on its right side
And the setting sun in his flying chariot
Warms the left.
        You would praise our climate. And if
You only knew that the bushes bear plums and
Red cornel berries, that the white oak and ilex
Make the cattle happy with acorns, and
Their master happy with shade? Why,
You would say that Tarentum had been brought
To bloom roundabout us. And a spring —
Worthy to give its name to a river
As cool and as pure as the Hebrus
That flows through Thrace — gives water
Good for headaches, good for the stomach!
This retreat so sweet — yes, if you believe me,
Enchanting — keeps me in good health during
The hot September days.

In his epistle to Lollius (Epis. I, xviii) he tells how his soul prospers in this secluded spot.

Does philosophy beget virtue, or does Nature bestow it? What is it that diminishes a man's cares, what will make him most self-content? Is it a successful political career, is it the pleasantness of gain, or a quiet pilgrimage along the path of life, unnoticed and unknown?

As for me, as often as the Digentia, the icy brook that supplies water to Mandela (a village wrinkled by the cold) makes me feel fresh and strong, what do you think my feelings are, what do you think I pray for? This is it. May I continue to have what I now have or even less! May I live as I like for what remains of my life (if the Gods will that aught remains)! May I have a good supply of books and provisions to last the year; and may I not vacillate, like a pendulum, between differing hopes for the dubious future!

It is enough to pray to Jupiter, who gives and takes away, that he grant me life and the means by which to live; a heart self-sufficient I myself will provide.

The Sabine farm was home to him, the dearest spot on earth, and though he liked other places, too, and enjoyed a visit to them, none, not even Tarentum, were ever real rivals.

IX

THE COUNTRY

I AM not sure that the preference of country to town is an article of the Epicurean creed, but it certainly was of Horace's. When he speaks of the city there is a note of peevishness; you might think him contrary, almost ill-tempered, he dislikes so much the noise, the bustle, and the pretense. And he appears to regard all the inhabitants except Maecenas and his circle as members of that *profanum vulgus* which excited his fastidious aversion. But in the country he shows himself as he is, cheerful, gay, good-humored, friendly, meditative, grateful, reverent, and composed. His dominant quality is the reverse of *accidie*. In the *Inferno* Dante comes upon souls that have committed the dreadful sin, *Non fummo lieti nel aer dolce*, "In God's sweet air we were not happy." That sin, while in the country, Horace never committed. Day by day in the great temple of Nature he worshipped the genius of Life, and expressed his gratitude by almost uninterrupted enjoyment, so thankful was he for health and luxury and verses and friends and his beloved farm.

You can almost hear him wending his way to Fons Bandusiae:

Benedicite, omnia opera Jovis Jovi!
Benedicite, nemora, sylvae, fontes, flores!
Benedicite, haedi, agnelli, boves, aves, canes!
Benedicite, puellae, Benedicite pueri!
Dianam tenerae dicite virgines
Intonsum, pueri, dicite Cynthium.

Blest be Sylvanus guardian of boundaries,
Blest be Priapus protector of gardens,
Pan, and our beloved Penates and Lares,
Makers of hearth and of home.

It is on his Sabine farm that the poet becomes sentimental, as sentimental as was possible for a Roman born on the borders of Apulia. He loves the ilex trees, the vineyards, the smell of the good brown earth, the sight of grazing cattle and browsing goats, and yet his thoughts easily wander off to the pageant of Roman glory and the great deeds of Roman heroes, and to the white throat of Glycera, or to Neaera's kisses. He becomes so sentimental at times that some people speak of him as religious, or superstitious, according to their personal conceptions of reality. I do not think either epithet correct. I do not think you can call a man superstitious who accepts the opinions of the wisest and most learned men of his time; nor do I think you can call Horace religious, if by religious you mean an abiding belief in spiritual powers beyond the reach of our senses.

He certainly was very grateful to have escaped death, which threatened him three times: at Philippi, in a shipwreck, and by a falling tree, and perhaps the impetuous rush of vital enthusiasm, which a sudden escape from death pours into the heart, affected him, as it does other men, with a sense of over-arching protection,

Di me tuenter, dis pietas mea
Et Musa cordi est,

and he often attributed benefits and blessings to various deities. His religion — if it will be allowed to be a religion — consisted in this attribution and in an emotional, romantic, affection for the traditional forms of worship and sacrifice. Beneath this pious behavior lay his love of nature, and of rural life: sentiment begetting love of form, and love of form in its turn begetting sentiment.

The most direct statement of his appreciation of the pleasures of country life, perhaps, is found in his second epode. The poet, as if to anticipate a mood of Heinrich Heine, puts these reflections in the mouth of Alfius, a moneylender:

> Happy the man who far above
> "The madding crowd's ignoble strife,"
> Like the primeval race of men,
> Plows his ancestral fields.
> No borrower nor lender he,
> No soldier by wild bugle called to arms,
> Nor does he shudder at the angry sea.
> He shuns the busy Forum
> And proud thresholds of prepotent men.
>
> Freely he twines about tall poplar trees
> His marriageable vines, or goes to view
> His lowing herds in far off valleys roam;
> Or prunes unfruitful branches with his knife,
> And grafts on healthier slips;
> In jars well-washed his liquid honey stores,
> Or shears his tender sheep,
> Or, when with ripe fruits garlanded
> Autumn has raised her ruddy head,
> How he delights to pick the grafted pears,
> And grapes that vie with purple dye,
> From which he will reward you, Priapus,
> And you, Silvanus, God of boundaries.

What joy to lie beneath the oak
Or on the matted grass,
While slowly glide between high banks
The waters of the brook,
And in the woods the sweet birds sing,
And flowing fountains murmurous
Invite the dewy-feathered sleep.

The poem continues this ideal picture of a farmer's life — temperate, simple, essentially Epicurean, free from politics and debt — and, at the end, Horace unexpectedly perpetrates a whimsical trick, as I say almost in the manner of Heine. He says, "When the moneylender Alfius had uttered these sentiments, he (the would-be farmer) calls in all his loans, and is now trying to put his moneys out again on usury." This bit of *gaminerie*, however, does not disturb the fact that the verses represent the poet's own feelings.

Sometimes Horace excused his leaving town for his farm on the plea that there he would have nothing to distract him, that he would be free to devote all his time to composition. He took with him for stimulants Menander, Archilochus, Eupolis, or others. But things did not turn out as he hoped, for even there, in the most advantageous circumstances, the *mollis inertia* laid hold of him, and the poet took life easy — he lay in the elm tree's shade, or *in remoto gramine* (Odes II, iii), or *sub arta vite* (Odes I, xxxviii), or *Dionaeo sub antro* (Odes II, i), or *sub laurea mea* (each spot had its separate excuse), and there he dozed a good deal, hummed "Lalage, my Lalage," and did not produce much verse (Sat. II, iii).

The trouble was that the outdoors offered too many distractions; he would think how pleasant it would be to have Quinctius Hirpinus out for a meal, *al fresco*, flowers, wine, and Lyde playing the lyre for them. Or, he might think of Pompeius Varus, the old friend who had fought at Philippi with him;

they would drink deep together as they had in the old days, for (Odes II, vii):

> . . . recepto
> dulce mihi furere est amico,

'Tis sweet to make mad holiday when a friend has been regained.

Dear to him in the summer, the country is also dear to him in winter. He admired Soracte, the high mountain to the north, its top white with snow; he admired the great trees with branches bending under their icy burdens, and the frozen rivers, and he delighted in the happy consequence that the wintry outdoors makes the warm indoors doubly agreeable. Pile logs on the fire! Fetch out a jug of mellowing wine, pour it very generously (Odes I, ix). Don't talk of other things! Come, let us anoint our heads with Assyrian perfumes, and cheer our hearts with music and song (Epode XIII).

But summer was the time that set his fancy at work, from the first budding of April leaves to their falling in October. It was then that the deities of the woods, fields, brooks, and fountains made their beneficent presences felt, giving strength to the oak, luxuriance to the vine, and bubbling ripples to the Digentia and the Anio. Some people, no doubt, have a taste for unity, people of orderly life, of dogmatic cerebration, whose minds are neatly cast in a one-chambered mould, who cheer for monotheism and revel in oneness. But others find the universe made up of an innumerable number of forces, find themselves enmeshed in multiplicity — of these was Horace. Jove, no doubt, was the supreme ruler of the universe, but that did not prevent lesser deities from performing acts of kindness to men, and Horace loved to feel that they took notice of him.

And as it is natural, when one feels gratitude, to wish to express it, he loved to take part in, at least to watch, the rites of building altars and offering sacrifices by which the country folk expressed their gratitude. His heart was wholly enlisted, and said "Amen" whenever a kid was sacrificed to the nymph of the *Fons Bandusiae,* or to Faunus, a sympathetic god, *Nympharum fugientium amator,* or when a simple oblation of meal and crackling salt was offered to the Household Gods in an honorable cottage (Odes III, xxiii). He loved to be present when young and old danced and sang and emptied the wine bowls, while the oxen rested in the fields and wolves left the sheep unharmed (Odes III, xviii). It was to the Goddess Diana, beautiful goddess, guardian of hill and grove, *montium custos nemorumque,* that he dedicated the pine tree which overhung his farm house (Odes III, xxii).

X

DESIPERE IN LOCO

Horace was an Epicurean. He says (Epis. I, iv):

> Me pinguem et nitidum bene curata cute vises,
> cum ridere voles, Epicuri de grege porcum.

> As for me, when you wish to laugh, you will find me fat,
> Sleek, well-washed and shaven, a pig from Epicurus' herd

Some scholars deny that he belonged to any sect. Some assert that he was as much a Stoic as an Epicurean. It is hard to find a disciple of any creed or philosophy who is perfectly consistent. Christians would like to hang their enemies, Mohammedans sometimes drink wine. Every man's creed is burdened by a penumbra of vague thought that contains elements of inconsistent doctrine. Horace was indeed an Epicurean, an admirable example of that worthy sect.

The confusion has arisen from a misconception of Epicurus' doctrine. If you think his disciples did not have their serious side, read Lucretius; if you think that their pleasures were primarily gross, read what Diogenes Laertius says of the master. When Horace said that he was a pig of Epicurus' herd, he described the pig as *nitidum bene curata cute*, with skin clean and fresh, something that the uncleanly, the profligate and debauched, never had. Epicurus was eminently fastidious; he said pleasure is the goal and guide of life, but he rated intellectual pleasures higher than physical pleasures. He permitted the primrose path, with the proviso that it should not interfere with the higher life. But to give a man a label in philosophy is quite superfluous.

Horace had had his fill of hardships during his service in Brutus' army, and a dull and dreary time on his return to Rome, until he made friends with Virgil and Varius. After lean years, fat years were welcome, and he liked to have a good time, not merely enjoying the country, the Sabine Hills, the soft southern warmth of Tarentum, the sparkling waves on Baiae's bay, or the pleasures of friendship, which he did with a vengeance, but also according to Luther's inspired phrase,

> Wer liebt nicht Wein, Weib und Gesang
> Bleibt ein Narr sein Leben lang.

I do not deny that Horace had a coarse side. Most men have, and there are two poems which English translators do not translate, but apart from those, almost every line may be presented *pueris virginibusque* without a qualm. Wine he appreciates (Odes I, xviii):

> Siccis omnia nam dura deus proposuit neque
> mordaces aliter diffugiunt sollicitudines.

To teetotallers God has ordained that all be hard, nor is there any other way to disperse cares than by wine.

In this same ode he bids his friend Varius, who had an estate at Tibur, plant no tree in preference to the vine; and when he invites Maecenas to visit the Sabine farm, it is not country air, fresh goat's milk, or homemade cheese that he holds out, but wine from the neighborhood (Odes I, xx).

When he escaped destruction by a falling tree, it was to Bacchus, protector of poetry, that he vowed a pure white goat, and in celebration of that anniversary (Odes III, viii), he invited Maecenas to empty his cup a hundred times. As to the hundred cups: in order to reassure us, Mr. Wickham says a hundred means an indefinite number, and to reassure you further I may add that the cup in question, the *cyathus*, is extremely small.

The poem (Odes III, xix) in which Horace proposes a toast to the newly elected augur, Murena, Maecenas' brother-in-law, describes something not readily distinguishable from high jinks. It seems that there was to be a Dutch treat. The poet complains that the proposed banqueters are conversing in highbrow fashion of learned matters, instead of coming to the point — at whose house the party is to be, and at what o'clock, and who is to see that the water is hot, and how much they shall pay for the Chian wine? When they do meet, anything serves for a toast: "Here's to the new moon," "Here's to midnight," "Here's to Murena!" And the poet interjects, *insanire juvat!* "What fun to have a high old time! Play the flute! Blow the pipe! Twang the lyre! Everybody do something! Scatter roses! . . . Telephus! Rhode is making up to you! And oh! how madly I am in love with Glycera."

I hasten to say that this is the most uproarious of his wine parties. For he really is strong for moderation even at jollifications: read his lines in Odes I, xxvii. It is the beneficence of wine that he praises: "Thou bringest back hope to troubled hearts, Thou givest courage to the poor man" (Odes III, xxi); "Blest be the jar that will generously bestow new hopes and

wash away the bitterness of care" (Odes IV, xii). Indeed, his
attitude is a rational rebuke to those silly misguided people who
would reject one of Nature's best gifts. Wine is indispensable
at a celebration. Horace was sure of that — "What is the best
thing to do on Neptune's feast day? Hurry, Lyde, bring out an
old bottle of Caecuban" (Odes III, xxviii). I need quote no
more. Horace was a rational creature and, grateful for the
spiritual fountain of mirth, jollity, friendship, and glee; he
counsels the moderate use of wine at every feast of rejoicing,
with a veiled suggestion that on days of triumph it is better to
err on the side of more rather than on the side of less. His appreciation of wine lies like morning dew on his poetry.

One would like to have notes on his wine cellar, though it
seems that he often had merely local wine on hand, ordering
the better wines from some vintner for special occasions and for
his fashionable friends. Here is a partial list of his wines:

Sabine, wine from his own vineyards, *vin ordinaire,* refreshing,
by no means to be despised.

Falernian, a richer wine from Campania of which there were several varieties, *austerum* or *severum* (a bit heady), and also
dulce (sweet), and *tenue* (mild).

Calenum, a wine from Cales, Campania, probably somewhat
similar to Falernian.

Caecuban, a dry wine from near Terracina, favored by the rich,
and drunk by Horace on festive occasions.

Formian, from vineyards at Formiae, about like Caecuban.

Chian, a sweet wine imported from the island of Chios — presumably expensive, sometimes used in luxurious sauces.

Lesbian, from the island of Lesbos, probably somewhat similar
to Chian wine, but mild; also a luxury.

Coan, wine from the island of Cos, a white wine apparently with some beneficial laxative effect.

Mareoticum, a strong sweet wine, made from white grapes from Marea, in the Delta in Egypt — though Horace knew of it, it does not appear that he had any in his cellar.

Massic, grown near Sinuessa in Campania, a stronger wine, that brought forgetfulness, *obliviosum.* In one of his satires (Sat. II, iv) Horace quotes a gourmet as saying, "If you set Massic under a clear sky, its coarseness will be toned down by the night air, and its unpleasant scent will pass off, whereas if it is strained through linen, it is spoiled and loses its full flavor."

Surrentine wine, grown at Sorrento, as to which the same gourmet advises mixing it with the lees of Falernian, and clearing it with the yolks of pigeons' eggs.

Veientanum, from vineyards at Veii, a cheap poor wine. It is probable that Horace himself did not drink it, but he may have given it to his slaves.

Alban, a strong wine of the better sort, that gained by keeping.

The cheaper wines were drunk when they were comparatively fresh, but the finer wines were of recorded vintage and kept for years, as, for instance, Massic of vintage 65 B.C.

One is glad that Horace was a worshipper, a moderate worshipper — good men usually are — of the benevolent God Bacchus, and wise men have ever been in agreement with him. Horace speaks of Cato (Odes, III, xxi) thus:

> Narratur et prisci Catonis
> saepe mero caluisse virtus.

> We are told that virtuous old
> Cato often grew warm with wine.

And Odysseus says:

I proclaim that there is no greater consummation of delight than when Joy fills a whole company who sit at a banquet in due order and listen to a minstrel, while tables before them are laden with bread and meat, and the cupbearer draws wine from the bowl and carries it around and pours it into the cups. This seems to me the most beautiful thing there is. (Odyssey, Book IX, lines 5–10).

The Miracle at Cana blessed this opinion.

XI

LA FEMME

Rixae, pax et oscula rubentis puellae.

I HEARD a song once which asserted that "The wisest King that ever lived, he dearly loved the lasses, oh!" To turn one's back wholly on the sex would surely be folly. True wisdom, I take it, lies somewhere in between, *aurea mediocritas*.

In Horace's time, at Rome, it was not the fashion among the gentry to marry for love. Women were not as well educated as men, and therefore less companionable. The poor married for the sake of children and to gain a housewife. The rich married for the sake of a dowry, or for an alliance with some person of political influence. Marriage for love was rare, although Augustus married for love, as did Maecenas. A man like Horace who enjoyed intelligent and cultivated conversation did not wish an uneducated woman in his house. He was essentially a man's man, a born celibate. He never thought of marrying, he was never in love; he never deceived himself as to the nature of his emotions; his soul was never touched.

There was of course a period in which he trod the primrose path, when he wore smart clothes, and his lustrous black hair grew low on his forehead, when he liked to rattle away and laugh in gay company, drink well-strained Falernian at midday, and, though he brought no gifts, found favor with Cinara (Epis. I, vii; I, xiv). But that was in the golden days of youth. As a middle-aged man he changed; in his riper years he learned to enjoy a modest meal and a nap on the grass beside the little river; and, as he says (Epis. I, xiv):

Nec lusisse pudet, sed non incidere ludum.

Shame does not lie in having played the fool
But in not cutting Folly short.

Horace mentions a goodly number of young women. They flit through his poems, fitful, charming, evanescent — flashes of light, and yet but shadowy figures. He gave them names, but I take it that none of the names are true. His generation was sufficiently like ours to make a rule that women's names should not be bandied about, even in poetry, and Roman gentlemen observed the rule. Virgil speaks of Cytheris, an actress and the mistress of Cornelius Gallus, under the name Lycoris; Catullus writes of Clodia as Lesbia; Propertius wrote of the woman he loved, whose real name was Hostia, under the name Cynthia, although she was a courtesan; Horace speaks of Terentia, Maecenas' wife, as Licymnia. What's in a name? What care we who was the lovely She "that wasted her time and Edmund Waller," or who Lucasta was, or Althea, or Saccharissa, or who the "one dear She" that was all the world to Abraham Cowley? It is of slight consequence now how much flesh and blood, and how much fancy, belonged to these girls in Horace's poems.

And not only are their names fictitious, but the girls themselves are but part real. It is not only in the poem of a poet that a ladylove is compounded of fact and fancy; no man knows where truth in his idol ends and fiction begins. Critics have argued for centuries as to how much of Dante's Beatrice was Divine Wisdom and how much a Florentine lady, and whether Petrarch's Laura ever lived or not. So Horace was quite justified in his portrayals; sometimes, no doubt, he borrowed from other poets, sometimes he set down happy memories, sometimes he sketched from dream girls that footed it beside him as he strolled along the banks of the Digentia or in the upland pastures, composing verses as he went.

But be that as it may, none of the names, none of the verses that contain them, suggest any depth of feeling. Depth of feeling he possessed, but that he kept for his friends.

These girls, half real as I say, half imaginary, differ in character and in class. If none were graced by the niceties of behavior required of a lady, I believe that some were as modest as if they had been, and I think very few deserved a coarse name. I will give you a list of them, a partial list, as they appear in his poems. One never can be sure of his chronology.

Inachia (Epode XI). The poet says to his friend Pettius,

It is now three years since I lost my infatuation for Inachia. Poor me! I am now ashamed of that episode. I was the talk of the town. I suffer at remembrance of dinner parties, at which my listlessness and my sighs betrayed how much in love I was. You remember how, after I had drunk some wine, I used to whine to you, "Does a true heart avail naught against money?" and then my anger boiling up I would cry out, "I will leave her, I will not struggle against rivals who are not my equals," and was pleased with myself and my austere purpose. And you would advise me to go home. But my irresolute steps carried me back to that unfriendly door, and that hard threshold.

Phryne (Epode XIV). Horace tells Maecenas that the reason why he has not finished a promised poem, long since begun, is that he is consumed by love for Phryne. One may put her in the same class as Inachia, but they were not harlots.

Neaera (Epode XV).

One night the moon shone in a cloudless sky among the lesser stars, and you, oh! Neaera! soon to prove false, clinging to me closer than ivy twines about an oak, vowed loyalty in the very words I asked. But if I have a spark of manhood left, I will not brook your giving your nights to a successful rival. In just anger I shall seek another mate, I will not let my grief subject me to your beauty.

And you, my rival, whoever you may be, triumphant, rich, handsome, you, too, will weep for her love when she transfers it to another, and I, in my turn, shall laugh."

Pyrrha (Odes I, v). This girl was fair-haired and a flirt, and, confident in her beauty, *simplex munditiis*, renounced ornaments. She had captivated Horace. Now some other wooer has caught her fancy. But, the poet says, her new lover who for the moment thinks her pure gold, and believes her constant, will experience oncoming storms and the treacherous sea. "I admit I have been shipwrecked. In the Temple to Neptune, you will find my dripping garments hanging on the wall, and a votive tablet recording my thanks to the God that saved me."

Leuconoë (Odes I, xi). Here is a much more stable attachment. "Ask not, Leuconoë — we cannot know — what date the Gods have set for you and me. . . . It is better to bear what comes . . . whether at the end of many years or now. . . . Love wisdom, strain the wine, and cut our high hopes according to the brevity of life. Even while we talk, old Time is still a-flying. Enjoy today, trust not tomorrow."

Lydia (Odes I, xiii). The poet is jealous, for Lydia praises Telephus for his beauty, and her lips,

> . . . quae Venus
> quinta parte sui nectaris imbuit,

"which Venus had imbued with the quintessence of her own nectar," bear the telltale marks of his drunken kisses. Horace warns her that there is no hope of constancy in such a fellow, and meditating on Lydia's faithlessness and Telephus' inconstancy, he adds the famous quatrain,

> felices ter et amplius,
> quos inrupta tenet copula nec malis
> divolsus querimoniis
> suprema citius solvet amor die.

"Thrice happy, and in greater measure, are they whom an unbroken bond holds together, whose Love unuprooted by wicked quarrels shall not dissolve before the day of death."

This reflection, born of contemplating quarrels and partings, almost leads Horace to that mood which Wordsworth expressed on listening to the stock dove:

> I heard a stock dove sing, or say,
> Its homely song the other day;
> It sang of love with quiet blending,
> Slow to begin and never ending,
> Of serious faith and inward glee,
> That was the song, the song for me.

Such moods Horace had, I am sure, but he never expresses them outright; you can at most catch a glimpse of one now and again, as in the following (Odes I, xvi), and you must keep eyes and heart open to recognize it.

> O matre pulchra filia pulchrior!

Who the lovelier daughter was we cannot guess. In his passionate youth the poet had in his anger said things that he was sorry for. Will she not forgive and forget?

Tyndaris (Odes I, xvii). Horace invites her to come to a shady nook in his retired valley, and to bring her lyre to accompany her songs; there they will drink mild Lesbian wine, quite out of sight of Cyrus (that unsuitable rowdy friend of hers), who is capable of pulling off her flowery coronal and tearing her clothes with his rude hands.

This ode gives a fair picture, I think, of what these young women usually were: they were fond of a kiss and fond of a guinea, girls that enjoyed country pleasures, singing and playing the lute, a cup of wine, men of good breeding, and yet had not the character, or the will, to keep rude boisterous lovers at arms' length.

Glycera (Odes I, xix). The poet confesses that he is again in love, to his own surprise, for he had thought such follies were ended. But Glycera's dazzling beauty, her charming flirtatiousness and her bewitching face have done the deed.

> in me tota ruens Venus,
>
> Down on me swoops Venus in all her power.

He bids his slaves set up an altar of grassy turf, lay myrtle leaves, bring forth incense and a bowl of wine, in hope to propitiate the goddess.

Lalage (Odes I, xxii). Her speech and laughter were so sweet to his ear, that as he walked in the wild woods, he only thought of her, and forgot that there might be wild animals about. Perhaps she is the same Lalage of Odes II, v, too young to marry yet, but sure of being loved more than was Pholoë the coquette, or Chloris, whose shoulders shone like the white moon upon a midnight sea. The lines are few but they have bestowed immortality.

Myrtale (Odes I, xxxiii). She is mentioned as a passionate girl, stormier than the Adriatic, once a slave, who held him in pleasant fetters when he should have been in love with a more presentable woman.

Galatea (Odes III, xxvii). This girl only appears upon our scene as she is going away to some foreign land, and Horace takes dispassionate leave of her,

> sis licet felix, ubicumque mavis,
> et memor nostri, Galatea, vivas,

> May you be happy, Galatea, wherever
> you are and do not forget me.

Cinara. One of the girls most talked about by the commentators, and some think that she was not imaginary. She appears several times, and Horace applied adjectives to her that are, vulgarly perhaps, said to be true to a man's attitude towards a girl that forsakes him, first she is "good" (*bona*, Odes IV, I), then she became "froward" (*proterva*, Epis. I, VII), and, after she had gone, "greedy" (*rapax*, Epis. I, XIV).

I have given enough of a list to show that life on the Sabine farm was not dreary, not without feminine blandishments. Was it not better to sport with Neaera in the shade than to waste one's life in the pursuit of office and popular applause? These girls were not in Roman society, but there was nothing unseemly in their little fêtes, nothing rowdy; they drank mild wine, and sang, and played on some musical instrument.

The following ode on Maecenas' birthday gives us a good idea of such an occasion (Odes IV, XI):

> Est mihi nonum superantis annum
> plenus Albani cadus.

I have a cask of Alban wine more than nine years old. In the garden, Phyllis, there is parsley for pleating a coronal, and there is a great growth of ivy; if you twine it in your hair, how lovely you will look. The house glitters with silver, the altar is decked with immaculate green leaves, and is quite ready for the sacrifice. The household is all of a skurry, men and maids run hither and thither helter-skelter. Fires are burning, the smoke goes rolling upwards.

You must know to what festival you are invited. We are going to celebrate the Ides of April, the day that divides in two the month of sea-born Venus, a day sacred for me, and to be observed almost more than my own birthday, because from this day my dear Maecenas reckons his passing years. . . . Come, Phyllis, come, Last of my Loves, for I shall never again be enamoured of a woman, learn a song to be sung by your lovely voice. The song will drive black care away.

XII

LYDE

O NE does not associate the young women I mentioned in the last chapter with thoughts of vice or grossness, and yet few, if any, rated chastity high. No wave of Puritanism had ever swept over Rome. They had never heard Miltonic preaching:

> So dear to Heav'n is saintly chastity,
> That when a soul is found sincerely so
> A thousand livried angels lackey her,

and if they had, they might have laughed at the sermon and the preacher. Nature had never preached like that to them when Pan and his troop, or Bacchus and his train, came piping and dancing over the Sabine Hills.

However, from the list of the young damsels that Horace has celebrated, there are two who attract me the most, who stand out as exceptional figures and present charming images of innocent maidenhood: Lyde and Lalage. Of the latter I have already spoken. Lyde appears three times, first, I think — for in publishing his odes Horace did not observe any strict chronological order — in Odes III, xi, secondly in Odes II, xi, and thirdly in Odes III, xxviii.

The first ode (Odes III, xi) I shall not attempt to explain, for the good reason that I do not understand it myself. It seems unusually free, even for Horace, of any normal sequence of ideas; some scholars have suggested that this is due to the influence of Pindar. But as our sole interest in the ode, at least for the moment, is due to Lyde, it is unnecessary to disentangle a rational linking of ideas. It begins with the poet's appeal to Mercury, the music-maker, to sing songs to which Lyde will incline her obstinate ears, for like the filly three years old she leaps and bounds over the broad fields exultant, and is frightened at a touch, too young to marry yet.

The second reference to Lyde is in Odes II, xi. A friend of the poet, Quinctius Hirpinus, apparently in the public service, perhaps an officer in the army, is troubled about the enemies of Rome: what the Scythians and Cantabrians, wild peoples who kept breaking the *Pax Romana,* might be doing. Horace reminds him that these enemies are separated from Italy by intervening seas, and bids him not bother about them. He adds, somewhat abruptly, that life needs little — that Youth and Beauty have their fingers ever at their lips bidding adieu, that gray hair is already driving away gallantry and childlike sleep, and that the flowers of Spring lose their glory.

Why rack your mind, Hirpinus, with insoluble problems of the future? A better way is to lie on the grass under one of my plane trees or a pine, perfume our grizzled heads with Assyrian nard, crown them with garlands of roses, and quaff care-dispelling wine. Water from the brook will temper the Falernian, if it should be too strong.

But Horace obviously felt that these preparations to cheer Hirpinus and give him a good time were inadequate. A crowning grace was lacking. It seems to me probable that he has already invited Lyde and that she is late, or that he fears she will be. The last stanza gives what explanation there is:

> Who will call the *devium scortum* from her house?
> Go bid her hurry and bring her ivory lyre,
> And if her hair is not done up, let her
> Knot it, after the mode of a Spartan maid.

Lyde is charming, for were she not, Horace would not be so zealous for her presence at this little picnic party for his friend. It is she, with her songs and her ivory lyre, that would make the statesman forget his worries. But there is an obstacle in our interpretation: those two words *devium scortum*. If one found them elsewhere in prose one would translate as "wayward harlot"; but any such translation here would most surely be wrong. It does not suit the picture. A touch of Teniers in a Watteau. Besides, that would be a hopeless contradiction to the earlier Lyde, the maiden filly of Odes III, xi. Professor Bennett translates the words as "coy wench." I should render the line thus: "Who will go fetch Lyde — [under his breath] the wayward baggage! — from her house?"

The word house (*domo*) confirms the hypothesis of modesty. Professor Bennett says it is her house, not Horace's, and therefore, acting on the theory that we are dealing with actual facts, I assume it to be the house of one of his tenants, a neighbor, with whom, especially as there was a pretty daughter, he was on terms of intimacy. This hypothesis is corroborated by the third ode (Odes III, xxviii). I will translate it:

> What better can I do for Neptune's fête?
> Hurry, Lyde, bring the Caecuban from the cellar,
> And make a breach in our barricaded sobriety.
>
> You see the sun hastens to its setting,
> But you stand as if the day stood still, and stingily

Delay to bring out from the store closet the jar
Waiting ever since Bibulus was consul.

In turn we will sing of Neptune and the sea-green
Locks of the Nereids; you shall sing in your turn,
On your curved lyre, of Latona and
The arrows of Diana swift of foot.

Our final song shall be of Her
Who rules Cnidos and the shining Cyclades,
And with her harnessed swans visits Paphos.
Night, too, shall be chaunted in appropriate song.

Lyde a trollop! Never! Would Horace ask any girl who
was not a modest maiden to sing a hymn to Diana, the maiden
Goddess? Only virgins sang hymns to Diana, *Dianam tenerae
dicite virgines!* (Odes I, xxi). And read the invocation to
Apollo and Diana in the *Carmen Saeculare* (the italics are mine):

O Phoebus, and Diana, Queen of the Woods, glorious splendor of the
heavens! O ye worshipped and ever to be worshipped, grant these our
prayers at this holy season, at which the Sybil has commanded *choice
virgins* and *chaste boys* to sing the hymn in honor of the Gods, in whose
eyes the Seven Hills have found favor.

And compare Catullus:

dianam pueri integri
puellaeque canamus,

Virgins and chaste boys,
Let us sing hymns to Diana.

Dear old Horace! It is pleasant to think that he had a charming young neighbor intimate enough to know where the Caecuban was stowed in his cellar, and who could be called on to fetch
her lyre and, upon request, entertain him and his friends with
songs. *Honi soit qui mal y pense.*

XIII

ACTIUM

AFTER the first book of Satires appeared in 35 B.C., Horace did not publish anything more until the second book of Satires about 30 B.C. The times certainly had not been propitious for concentration upon poetry. Although Rome was at peace, the relations between Octavius and Mark Antony created uneasiness and disturbed the thoughts of the serious citizens. Patricians generally favored Antony, but the Equestrian Order and the lower classes inclined to Octavius. He had done well in Rome. He had shown his piety by restoring neglected temples and building new ones; he had manifested his care of the poor, who suffered most from robbers and fires, by establishing a police force and a fire brigade; and he had reduced taxes. One of his generals restored order in Africa; another, Messala Corvinus, quieted the turbulent Salassi in Piedmont; he himself conducted campaigns in Croatia and Dalmatia and brought under Roman domination the whole east coast of the Adriatic. These wars were of no great consequence, but they gave the citizens of Rome a pleasant sense of security. The black clouds on the horizon lay to the East.

These clouds were caused not only by the incompatible ambitions of two high-spirited men, but even more by the cleavage between East and West, between two ways of life, two ideologies. And in this cleavage a remarkable woman played a great part: Cleopatra, a Ptolemy of Greek blood, Queen of Egypt. Years before, she had captivated the "mightiest" Julius, and on his return to Rome had accompanied him, and had dwelt in a villa in his gardens across the Tiber. It seems that she had not deigned to conciliate public opinion. "I hate the Queen," Cicero said, and probably expressed the opinion of conservative Roman society. But Julius Caesar had not flaunted his relations with the Queen, whereas Mark Antony, whether he loved most the wealth of Egypt, or Cleopatra's beautiful body, or her infinite variety that "age could not wither nor custom stale," proclaimed his infatuation to all the world. He did what she wished, gave her great gifts — even territories belonging to the Roman Empire — and finally, in order to marry her, divorced Octavius' sister Octavia, whom he had married for the purpose of creating a bond of brotherhood. Insult could hardly go farther.

Octavia was a noble and lovely woman, and in Roman eyes stood as a symbol of what Romans admired in womanhood. Every Roman felt his share in the insult, and national patriotism flared up. The sober-minded West rose up against the lascivious East, and whatever remained of Roman traditions of family life, of private morality and public decency, blazed up in an angry flame.

For two generations and more the horrors of civil war, of proscriptions, of dictatorships, had driven to cover lovers of peace — the humble, the timid, men primarily interested in their own affairs, like Horace's father, men without ambition for office and yet, many of them, men of personal dignity and self-respect. These, peace had brought out of their hiding-places. They were shocked and disgusted by the voluptuous East, they despised the sly, crafty, oily ways of the Egyptians and Syrians. Horace says, *Persicos odi apparatus*, "I hate oriental luxuries." So did many of his fellow citizens, and they were ready to fight for the preservation of their old way of life.

In Cleopatra they saw the embodiment of the licentious, malevolent, dishonorable East; they believed that she, drunk with prosperity, *fortuna dulci ebria*, was plotting the ruin of the Capitol and the destruction of the Roman state; they loathed her counsellors, "her polluted crew of shameless creatures"; they scorned the Roman legionaries, taken prisoners, who were willing to serve a woman and do the bidding of eunuchs. Nevertheless, the terror of imminent civil war frightened Rome. Horace wrote the epode, *Quo, quo scelesti ruitis?* "To what ruin, wretches, go ye?" and followed it up with another, *Suis et ipsa Roma viribus ruit*, "Rome of her own strength rushes to ruin."

The clouds grew blacker; quiet citizens were aghast. And then Mark Antony, "a great man, as Seneca said, turned to un-Roman ways by his love of drink and of Cleopatra," took the fatal step. With fleet by sea and army by land, accompanied by the bewitching Queen, he proceeded in hostile quest towards Italy, and reached the promontory of Actium at the mouth of the Ambracian Gulf in western Greece. There Octavius with his fleet came to meet him.

Virgil has described the situation (Aeneid, VIII): On one side, high on his ship stood Augustus Caesar, supported by all the Gods great and small, by the Fathers, and the People. On the other side, Antony with barbaric wealth, and soldiers of all sorts recruited from the peoples of the East, from Egypt, the remoter Orient, and far off Bactria, and O shame! his Egyptian wife followed him. Gods joined in the fight:

omnigenumque deum monstra et latrator Anubis
contra Neptunum et Venerem contraque Minervam
tela tenent.

Barking Anubis and monstrous gods of all sorts
Brandish their weapons against Neptune and Venus
And Minerva.

It was indeed a time of decision. On September 2 the two
navies joined in conflict. For a time the issue was in doubt.
Then on a sudden Cleopatra gave the signal of fear, and she and
all her galleys fled. Antony followed her. The victory was complete. Rome breathed freely. And the next year still more
comfortable news came: Antony had died upon his sword, and
the magnificent Queen had laid an asp to her breast. Rome went
wild with triumph. Virgil says:

laetitia ludisque viae plausuque fremebant,

The streets were in a frenzy of joy, and shouts
And jubilation.

Horace, too (Odes I, xxxvii), added his shout of exultation:

Nunc est bibendum, nunc pede libero
pulsanda tellus!

Now we must drink, now we must beat
The ground with light feet!

But even in the mad joy of relief from fear — though no
Roman could then do justice to that fascinating, enigmatical,
sly, crafty, wild, wanton personality — Horace felt a human
pride in Cleopatra's choice of death rather than life and the
gracing of Caesar's triumph. No cringing woman she, *non
humilis mulier!* After sixteen hundred years the divine lord of
language, creator of shapes more real than living men, did her

justice. Reread *Antony and Cleopatra,* and then you will understand the situation which I have tried to indicate.

I have read that "it is generally accepted by scholars that Horace was present at the Battle of Actium." If that is correct, it was an important fact in his life. The real question is, Was Maecenas present? for if not there is no reason to suppose that Horace was. Let us examine the evidence, which consists, I understand, solely of a statement by Dio, the Greek historian, and of inferences from two Epodes, I and IX.

Dio says that Maecenas was in charge of Rome during the campaign, and Buchan and Gardthausen accept this testimony. But Epode I clearly implies a plan for Maecenas to board a ship and take part in the war. This makes a possible but not necessary contradiction. The seeming disagreement may easily be reconciled by the assumption that Maecenas' plans were changed and that he did not go. It is quite possible that Octavius ordered him to stay in Rome.

Octavius crossed the sea to Epirus early in the year 31 B.C. The battle was fought on September 2. After the battle Octavius went on to Greece and wintered in Athens. Maecenas, almost certainly, was not with Octavius all that time; and it is difficult to suppose that he, not a soldier but a statesman and diplomat, described by his enemies as a fop, went to Actium merely for the fight. But, suppose that Maecenas did go, that need not mean that Horace went too.

Epode I begins:

Maecenas, my friend, you are going, ready to share every danger with Caesar in a [little] Liburnian galley against monstrous ships. But what of me, to whom life is a delight so long as you are with me, but without you a heavy burden? Shall I obey your orders to stay at ease, which will have no savor without you, or shall I follow you to hardship? You ask, seeing that I am not strong and far from warlike, if my endurance of hardship would help you. I answer that I shall suffer less fear for you if I am with you than if I were away. . . . I will gladly go to battle now and always in hope of your favor, but not in order to have you bestow upon me more, for you already have given me enough and more than enough.

It is plain that Horace expects Maecenas to go, but there is no further evidence that he did go (except what may be contained in Epode IX). It is also plain that Horace was more than willing to go with Maecenas, but he admits that he has been ordered (*jussi*) to stay behind. And why should Maecenas have taken Horace, *imbellis ac firmus parum*, to a naval battle in which he would be of no use? It was no pleasure trip. Octavius' Liburnian galleys were of "light build modelled on the piratical vessels of the Liburni, a tribe on the Illyrian coast." They were made for fighting, not for carrying civilian passengers.

Let us now see what Epode IX says. I will quote Professor Bennett's translation:

When happy Maecenas, within thy lofty palace — such is Jove's pleasure — shall I with thee, in joy at Caesar's triumph, drink the Caecuban stored away for festal banquets, while flute and lyre make music with their mingled melody of Phrygian and Dorian strains? Just as lately, when the Neptunian leader [Sextus Pompeius], his ships consumed, was driven from the sea in flight, though he had threatened the city with shackles he had taken from faithless slaves, his friends! The Roman, alas! (ye, O men of after times, will deny the charge) — the Roman bears stakes and weapons at a woman's behest, and a soldier, can bring himself to become the minion of withered eunuchs, while amid the soldiers' standards, the sun shines on the shameful Egyptian pavilion. At sight of this, twice a thousand Gauls, chanting the name of Caesar, turned away their snorting steeds; and the ships of the foe, when summoned to the left [*sinistrorsum citae*], lay hidden in the harbour! Io, Triumphe! [Hail! O God of Triumph] Dost thou keep back the golden cars and the unsullied kine? Io, Triumphe! Neither in Jugurtha's war didst thou bring back so glorious a captain; nor was Africanus such — he whose valour reared for him a shrine o'er

Carthage. Vanquished on sea and land, the foe has changed the scarlet
cape for sable, and against baffling winds is either making for Crete famed
for her hundred cities, or is seeking the Syrtes by Notus tossed, or is borne
upon uncertain seas. Bring hither, lad, more generous bowls, and Chian
wine or Lesbian, or pour out for us Caecuban, to check our rising qualms
[nausea]. 'Tis sweet to banish anxious fear for Caesar's fortunes with
Bacchus' mellow gift.

In interpreting this disjointed poem the old theory had been
that Horace was at home, perhaps on his Sabine farm, when news
of victory came, and there, in his enthusiasm, wrote the verses.
To this theory I subscribe. But, as I learn from Mr. Wickham's
notes, two learned German scholars, Herr Bücheler and Herr
Plüss, rejected that view, and argued "with great force and ingenuity" that the poem was written for an extempore banquet
on board Maecenas' Liburnian galley on the very night of the
battle, and that, therefore, the poet was on board and saw the
battle with his own eyes. The word nausea lies at the base of
their hypotheses. This word impressed the German scholars as
charged with a load of realism. They seem to have thought that
its employment ("a coarse touch," as Mr. Wickham observes)
indicates that the poet referred to his own feelings. And, argu-
ing on their side, Wickham holds that the phrase *sinistrorsum
citae* indicates an eye witness. (I foresee that hereafter some
scholar will argue that "cannon in front of them" suggests that
Tennyson accompanied the Light Brigade at Balaklava, and that
"cannon to right of them, cannon to left of them," clinched the
argument.) Wickham adds: "The precision of some details
combined with vagueness in the general picture, all suit a writer
close to the scene of action, who sees a part clearly but not the
whole, rather than one who hears news at a distance. . . . On
the decisive question whether Horace was actually present at
Actium or not, we have no conclusive evidence."

But, on the hypothesis that Horace was present, what happened? How do Herr Bücheler and Herr Plüss explain the sudden and unexpected cry,

> io triumphe, tu moraris aureos
> currus et intactas boves?

> Hail, God of Triumph, dost thou keep back
> The golden cars and the unsullied kine?

On this Wickham comments: " 'Triumphus' is personified. . . . There is an emphasis on 'tu' " with the implied meaning, " 'It must be the Triumph-god himself that delays the starting of the procession, all else is ready.' " But, if the battle is barely over and Horace and Maecenas are on the Liburnian galley, it would appear premature and unjust to impute blame to the Triumph-god for delay in fetching forth the golden chariots and the virgin heifers. Those surely must wait till Octavius could get back to Rome. Besides, Suetonius says: "The naval engagement near Actium was prolonged to so late an hour that after the victory Caesar was obliged to sleep on board his ship." Caesar may have been annoyed with the Triumph-god for delaying the procession, but he would have been still more annoyed to hear the Triumph-god bid him jump out of his berth and into the golden chariot and whip up virgin heifers.

John Buchan in *Augustus* says: "Octavian . . . waited all night at sea, rescuing men from the burning hulls, and in the morning returned to the gulf to discover the situation there. He found that the opposition was melting fast. The fleet was gone, but for some days the army under Canidius held its ground, though the desertion of its general had broken its spirit. Presently Canidius fled to Antony in Egypt, and the legions surrendered to Octavian." The situation that night would most assuredly have rendered a banquet on Maecenas' ship, graced by a poem, highly untimely. Besides, the poet says, *Terra marique victus hostis*, "the enemy defeated on land and sea," whereas the army on land did not surrender for seven days (Plutarch). This surely contradicts the Bücheler and Plüss theory.

The poem taken literally depicts the enemy as fleeing in many directions, while Horace and his company are revelling in triumph, and Horace cries out: "Steward! fetch hither bigger bowls, and Chian wine or Lesbian wine, or pour out Caecuban to quell our mounting nausea." Herr Plüss and Herr Bücheler, as I say, were impressed by this seasickness, but I am more impressed by the notion of seasick passengers calling for fuller cups of Chian and Lesbian, both sweet wines, or, as an antidote to nausea, Caecuban. No host, or steward, in his senses would serve sweet wines in a tossing sea. Besides, what purser, making provision for a sea-fight, that was to decide the fate of an empire as well as that of all hands on board, would store a Liburnian galley with imported wines? And surely, surely, if Horace and Maecenas were sitting seasick in the hold, while ships were blazing far and near, and men drowning, the last reflection to enter the poet's mind would be (however appropriate it might be if he were at his farm):

> curam metumque Caesaris rerum juvat
>   dulci Lyaeo solvere.

> It does one good to banish care and fear
> For Caesar's fortunes with sweet wine.

If Herr Plüss and Herr Bücheler had ever crossed the English Channel in stormy weather, they would have found it a mistake to call for Tokay, or Haut Sauternes, or Orvietano bianco; and they would not have said, "How delightful to banish care with sweet wine." Nor would they have thought it likely that seasick Horace would sit down and write a poem.

The Bücheler-Plüss theory has, I am told, the support of an

elegiac poem, of uncertain date, on the death of Maecenas; but a fanciful poet may easily, in his hastiness, have drawn the inference from the two epodes. The simplest theory is that Horace was at his Sabine farm, and on getting the happy news wrote his poem, rendering it reasonably verisimilar, and sent it to Maecenas in Rome, and that neither of them was at the sea-fight. In this way we do not contradict Dio.

XIV

SATIRES, BOOK II

AFTER Actium the next milestone in Horace's life was the publication of his second book of Satires. This book is said "to reveal a deeper concern for social and ethical problems." To my mind satire is an unattractive branch of literature. Why go about castigating one's fellow men, leaving unanswered the awkward question concerning the beam that gets into some eyes? It can hardly rate as poetry, and Horace never pretends that it does. Perhaps it aids the police, the clergy, and public opinion, in keeping wayward humanity within bounds. I know that the Hebrew satirists, Hosea and Habbakuk and their brethren were very respectable — like French *pères de famille* — that Juvenal, Boileau, and Dr. Johnson are high sounding names, and that all were great faultfinders. But such belaborings are displeasing to the belabored, and only give fitful pleasure to the belaboreds' friends and acquaintances, boring everybody else. Two great passages, Dryden on Zimri and Alexander Pope on Atticus stand out brilliantly, but to all else I have read of satire I am unsympathetic, and I cannot claim any exception for Horace's satires, I mean those that we call *Satires*, for his *causeries* are delightful and not at all what we call satire. So, I shall content myself with a sort of running index, hasty advice to readers to skip all compositions in the book but one.

No. I answers criticism made upon Horace's first book of Satires.

No. II asserts the superiority of plain living, especially of plain eating, to luxury and gluttony.

No. III tells how Horace listens to Damasippus relating the substance of a lecture delivered by a Stoic philosopher on avarice, ambition, self-indulgence and superstition. I find it very tedious.

No. IV is tolerably amusing. It consists of a dialogue between Horace and his acquaintance Catius, in which the latter expatiates on culinary matters: oblong eggs have a better flavor than round eggs; cabbages grown in dry places are better than those grown in a watered garden; if a friend drops in unexpectedly and the fowl be tough, a good expedient is to plunge it alive into diluted Falernian; mushrooms from the meadow are best; it is not a good plan to mix honey with strong Falernian; limpets and common shellfish are beneficial in case of constipation, but they must be accompanied by white Coan wine. And so on.

No. V deals with legacy hunting.

No. VI I have already quoted in part and shall come back to.

No. VII is a dialogue in which Horace's slave Davus uses the liberty allowed at the Saturnalia to speak his mind, and deliver an ironical Stoic sermon on the text that only the wise are free.

No. VIII describes a dreadfully dull dinner party at the house of one Nasidienus Rufus, to which even the fact that Maecenas is present cannot give a glimmer of interest.

There are eight poems in all, and, to my mind, with the exception of No. VI and perhaps No. IV, they should be left unread.

Satire VI is very pleasant, a glittering exception to the general dullness. I have already quoted the beginning, *Hoc erat in votis* and the description of the Sabine farm, but the whole is so characteristic of Horace that I shall now go ahead and quote much of the rest of it. It reveals more of his relations with Maecenas, and shows his love of country life. It is a sort of open letter, dated at his farm.

Well, now that I have transferred myself from Rome to my castle in the Sabine hills, what shall my pedestrian Muse first celebrate? Here, no wretched political ambition treads me down, nor the leaden sirocco, nor grievous autumn that makes a fat graveyard.

O Janus, Father of the morning, who starts men on the routine of life, I begin my song with you. At Rome you hurry me off to be surety! "Come, stir your stumps, lest somebody get ahead of you." So, go I must, in spite of the north wind and short snowy winter days. Then after I have assumed a risky obligation, I must push my way through the crowd and elbow aside the slow walkers. Some rude fellow curses and cries, "What the deuce do you want, you lunatic, what are you trying to do? I suppose you have suddenly remembered an engagement at Maecenas', and will knock down everything in your way!" And I will not deny that I am pleased by this accusation, indeed, it is honey-sweet to me.

As soon as I reach the once gloomy Esquiline Hill, a hundred petitioners press their concerns upon me. One says, "Roscius begs you to meet him at Libo's Well in the Forum before seven o'clock." Another one: "Horace! The treasury clerks beg you to remember to come back today on a new important matter that affects us all." A third: "Please get Maecenas to put his seal to these papers." If I say, "I'll try," the petitioner insists, "Oh, you can if you will."

It is now seven years or nearer eight since Maecenas included me among his friends, I mean such friendship as liking to take me along in his carriage on a drive and talk of trifles. "What o'clock is it?" "Is the Thracian chicken a match for Syrus?" "This cold morning nips people who are not careful," — and such things as may be safely confided to a leaky ear.

For all these years, yours to command has become more and more an object of envy. If I have been to the games with Maecenas, or played ball with him on the Campus, everybody cries out, "Oh, you lucky fellow!" If an alarming rumour runs through the city, everybody I meet asks me what I think of it, "My dear man, what have you heard about the Dacians? You must know, you are so near the powers that be." I answer, "I know nothing," to which they say, "Oh, why will you always be joking?" I repeat, "The deuce take me if I have heard a word." But they go on, "Does Caesar intend to settle his disbanded soldiers in Sicily or Italy?" And when I swear I know nothing, they look at me as at a man of most extraordinary reticence.

In this way my day is wasted, in spite of my prayers, "O when shall I see thee, dear Sabine farm! When shall I enjoy old books, and sleep, and idleness, and drink in sweet forgetfulness of care? Oh, when shall beans and greens dressed with bacon fat be served on my own table! Oh! When we dine in my house (leaving the remnants to saucy slaves) that is a feast fit for the Gods! Free from Bacchanalian rules each guest may as he pleases empty a big cup or a little, according as he has a strong head or prefers a mild glass. Then conversation follows, not gossip about villas and estates, or whether Lepos the actor dances well or ill, but upon matters of real concern, about which we ought to have ideas — Whether it is virtue or wealth that makes men happy, whether self-interest or righteousness leads to acts of kindness, and what is the nature of good and what its highest form.

In the midst of such talk our neighbor Cervius breaks in with an old wives' tale much to the point. For instance, someone praised the wealth of Arellius without realizing what anxieties wealth brings. Cervius began:

"Once upon a time, the story goes, a country mouse invited a city mouse to his poor dwelling, a mere hole. The two were old friends. The country mouse led a rough life and kept a close eye on what he had, nevertheless on occasion he would loose the strings of his parsimonious soul with acts of hospitality. He grudged neither vetch nor oats, and brought forth dried raisins and half-eaten bits of bacon, in hopes, by variety of fare, to overcome his friend's fastidiousness — for the latter hardly touched a morsel with his dainty tooth. The master of the house stretched himself out on fresh straw, ate spelt and darnel, and refrained from the choicer dishes of the feast.

"At last the city mouse said to the country mouse, 'I say, old boy, how can you bear to live this hard life on this steep wooded hill? Surely you must prefer city life and city people to this wild forest? Take my advice, come back with me. All creatures are mortal, neither great nor small escape death, therefore, old fellow, be happy while you may, have a good time, remember how short life is.' These words greatly impressed the country mouse, and he left his house with alacrity. Both took the road proposed, desirous of arriving in the city in the dark.

"And now Night was enthroned in the zenith of the heavens when the two entered a stately mansion in which scarlet covers shone on ivory couches, and masses of viands, left over from the evening's feast, were lying nearby in heaping baskets. So, when the city mouse had ensconced the country mouse at full length on a dark red cover, he bustled about like an approved waiter, and served course after course, performing the domestic duties of a slave, first tasting everything he served. The country mouse, lying at ease, enjoyed his new experience of good cheer, and enacted well the role of a delighted guest, when on a sudden a great noise from the door bounced both of them from the sofa. In terror they ran across the room and almost dead with fright trembled to hear the great house ring with the bark of Molossian hounds.

"The country mouse remarked: 'Good-by, I have no use for a life like this. My wood, my hole safe from attack, and a little vetch are good enough for me.' "

Perhaps La Fontaine told the fable better, but I do not think any of La Fontaine's lines happier than

Cupiens varia fastidia cena
vincere tangentis male singula dente superbo.

SATIRES, BOOK II

XV

THE EPODES

THE Epodes were probably published in 29 B.C., about a year after the second book of Satires. The word epode is the technical name applied to the shorter verse of a particular couplet, and from that to a poem made up of such couplets. The Greek poet Archilochus, I am told, first used it. Horace himself calls the verses *iambi*, because most of them are in iambic meter, a short syllable followed by a long. Of these poems there are seventeen.

During these years his position as a poet had become secure, and he felt free to abandon the hexameter verse familiar to the Romans, and introduce various Greek meters which he had learned at Athens. In grace and elegance of workmanship the Epodes are much inferior to the Odes; their chief interest lies in the personal references to the poet himself and to Maecenas, and to martial and political events of the time. In this period, as I have said, great transformations were shaping. The two masters of the world were at variance, and it was becoming clearer month by month that their differences could only be settled by the overthrow of one or the other. Of that I have spoken at some length in earlier chapters. Here I will merely give you a rough notion of the contents of the epodes.

Epode I concerns the plan that Maecenas should join Octavius' fleet at Actium, and I have already quoted from it at length.

Epode II describes the pleasures of country life, and is put into the mouth of Alfius, the moneylender. I have already quoted most of this.

Epode III is the merry one on garlic addressed to *Jocose Maecenas*.

Epode IV deals, in bad taste, with a vulgar *nouveau riche*.

Epode V describes the witch Canidia, whom we have met in the Satires, and her utensils: funereal cypresses, eggs of night-roving screech owl, blood of toad, poisonous herbs, bones snatched from the jaws of a starving bitch, and in general her black magic.

Epode VI threatens a threatener. An episode about which we know nothing. It is dull.

Epode VII seems to have been written under the dread of civil war:

Quo, quo scelesti ruitis?

Has too little Roman blood been shed on land and sea? And now will you draw swords, not against Carthaginians or Britons or Parthians, but against Rome herself?

The time is not indicated, but I have assumed that it was composed during the years before Actium.

Epode VIII is gross, and never translated in modern editions.

Epode IX is about the Battle of Actium. I have already discussed it.

Epode X holds up the name of Maevius to immortal contumely. In mock heroic style the poem expresses the hope that "the stinker Maevius" will be drowned on the voyage which he is about to embark on. It is poor in every aspect.

Epode xi I have quoted in Chapter XII.

Epode xii, like No. viii, is gross and left untranslated. The two stand like lepers outside the town walls.

Epode xiii is gay: Outdoors there is dirty weather (*horrida tempestas*) let's profit by it! Age shall not cloud the brow, fetch out the wine bottled when Torquatus was consul. To free our hearts from dire anxiety let us anoint our heads with Persian nard and cheer up our hearts with Mercury's lyre!

Epode xiv, in which Horace explains to Maecenas why he has not finished a promised poem, I have already quoted.

Epode xv, on faithless Neara, begins with the pretty lines

> Nox erat et caelo fulgebat Luna sereno
> inter minora sidera.

Epode xvi is a sort of continuation of No. vii with its lamentation over the horrors of civil war, and in a glow of imagination ends with an invocation to abandon Italy and escape to the Happy Isles, where men shall find the Golden Age restored.

Epode xvii concerns Canidia the witch, a subject eminently skippable (see Sat. I, viii; Epode V).

As you see, I am giving advice to skip. Only dilettanti are privileged to do this, for scholars can not. One definition of a scholar is a man who dares not skip. There is between the scholar and the dilettante the eternal contrast between the ant and the grasshopper. And oh, how the grasshopper skips! Let me whisper in your ear, reader, that the latter is the warier animal.

XVI

THE ODES

After the victory at Actium came the great work of organizing the Empire and installing the dictator Octavius as the Emperor Augustus. During these years Horace was busy with his Odes — *carmina* he called them. He had been working on them in his leisurely fashion for long years. He was in no hurry. As an Epicurean and as an artist, he did not believe in haste. In 23 B.C. the three books were published together and were a tremendous success; the author was justified in closing the volume with the famous ode that expresses his confidence in immortal renown:

> Exegi monumentum aere peronnius. . . .
> Non omnis moriar
>
> I have built a monument more enduring than bronze,
> Loftier than the royal pile of the pyramids;
> No devouring rain, nor the north wind's furious rages
> Can cast it down, nor series of innumerable years,
> Nor flight of ages. Not all of me shall die.

We can well believe that the poet was very happy in those seven years or more between Actium and the publication of the Odes — spending his summers at his Sabine farm, his winters in Rome, with visits perhaps to Plancus and Varus at Tibur, and trips to the delightful neighborhood of Baiae's bay, or in the environs of Tarentum. And wherever he was, one may suppose that he had his writing materials within handy reach in case he should be minded to compose a poem to one or another of his friends.

During that time his interest in his art became much more absorbing, in choice of word, in turn of phrase, in sequence or in contrast of ideas. He employed nineteen meters, and it is no easy matter to write a Latin poem in a Greek meter. The ancients wrote their poetry in meters composed of feet of long and short syllables: an iambus ∪ —, a trochee — ∪, a dactyl — ∪ ∪, a spondee — —, and so on. Of course only such words could be used as had syllables of proper lengths to fit into the prescribed scheme. Doing this was not only an art, but also great fun. Let me illustrate by means of the ninth ode in Book I, *Vides ut alta stet nive candidum Soracte.*

Horace sat down to write a poem about winter in Alcaic meter. He wished to say, "Do you see how Mount Soracte stands in deep snow, how the struggling trees can no longer bear their burden, and how the rivers are frozen by the bitter cold?" So he had to think up Latin words with long and short syllables fit for his purpose, and then arrange these words according to the meter which Alcaeus had used for his Greek words. This required ingenuity and taste. It resulted in this polished stanza:

$$\underset{\text{Vi}}{\cup} \mid \underset{\text{des}}{—} \; \underset{\text{ut}}{—} \mid \underset{\text{al}}{\cup} \; \underset{\text{ta}}{—} \mid\mid \underset{\text{stet}}{—} \; \underset{\text{ni}}{\cup} \; \underset{\text{ve}}{\cup} \mid \underset{\text{can}}{—} \; \underset{\text{di}}{\cup} \mid \underset{\text{dum}}{\cup}$$

$$\underset{\text{So}}{—} \mid \underset{\text{rac}}{—} \; \underset{\text{te,}}{\cup} \mid \underset{\text{nec}}{—} \; \underset{\text{iam}}{—} \mid\mid \underset{\text{sus}}{—} \; \underset{\text{ti}}{\cup} \; \underset{\text{ne}}{\cup} \mid \underset{\text{ant}}{—} \; \underset{\text{o}}{\cup} \mid \underset{\text{nus}}{—}$$

$$\breve{\;} \;\underline{\;} \;\breve{\;}\;\underline{\;}\;\underline{\;}\;\breve{\;}\;\breve{\;}$$
sil | vae la | bo ran | tes, ge | lu que

$$\underline{\;}\;\breve{\;}\;\breve{\;}\;\underline{\;}\;\breve{\;}\;\breve{\;}\;\underline{\;}\;\breve{\;}\;\breve{\;}$$
flu mi na | con sti te | rint a | cu to?

You can see what fun it was, a capital intellectual puzzle, and also why Horace did but little at a time, and let frequent intervals of idleness slip in between bouts of work, and you will also understand how Maecenas bothered him to death by constantly asking,

Mollis inertia cur tantam diffuderit imis
oblivionem sensibus,

as Horace relates in Epode xiv.

Horace composed when the spirit moved him, when some occasion caught his fancy. He was, we must allow, lazy. He enjoyed his farm, the pine tree's shade in summer, crackling flames on the hearth in winter; the company of friends, four-year-old Falernian, Lyde's ivory lyre, and Phryne's kisses; and he also loved his art, and practised it proudly, and laboriously, and intermittently. To me his art seems more like that of the architect than that of the musician; he does not care greatly for harmonious sounds, rather he is inspired by an architectonic sense of putting words in the right places, as if they were blocks of stone to make a cornice or a frieze, or voussoirs in an arch, or like tesserae in a mosaic. It was the Roman way.

The three books of Odes are arranged, the critics say, in a definite order, but not chronologically. The first ode in the first book is dedicated to Maecenas, the second to Augustus, the third to Virgil, the fourth to Sestius; the fifth is to a flirt, and the sixth to Agrippa. At any rate, the sequence, whatever it is, gives a would-be expositor of Horace's genius, wisdom, and lovableness, complete freedom in the order of reviewing the Odes.

I will now quote two characteristic odes from Book I. First No. XXII, because of its Horatian humor. It is addressed to his friend Aristius Fuscus:

> Integer vitae scelerisque purus
> non eget Mauris jaculis neque arcu
> nec venenatis gravida sagittis,
>   Fusce, pharetra,
> sive per Syrtis inter aestuosas
> sive facturus per inhospitalem
> caucasum vel quae loca fabulosus
>   lambit Hydaspes.

> The perfect man, untouched by guilt,
> Does not need Moorish javelins, nor bow,
> Nor quiver with poisoned arrow laden, Fuscus;
> Whether he wend his way
> Through the surging Syrtes or
> The churlish Caucasus or regions where
> The storied Hydaspes flows.

So far the verses are stately, formal, somewhat pompous, almost Johnsonian, and you expect the same strain to continue, in praise of virtue and an over-arching providence, when the poet suddenly discloses a wholly unexpected set of premises from which he had drawn the foregoing pious inferences:

> Namque me silva lupus in Sabina,
> dum meam canto Lalagen et ultra
> terminum curis vagor expeditis,
>   fugit inermem;
> quale portentum neque militaris
> Daunias latis alit aesculetis
> nec Jubae tellus generat, leonum
>   arida nutrix.

> Because while I was wandering in the Sabine woods,
> Beyond my boundaries, care left behind,
> Without a weapon, singing songs of Lalage,
>   A wolf fled from me!
> A monster such as warlike Apulia
> With her broad oak forests never breeds,
> Nor Numidia's desert land,
>   nurse of lions.

The reader is still dubious; Horace may have had a narrow escape, and in his gratitude, as unbelieving men often do, may be wondering if it might not be that Providence has spared him because of his righteousness, but then he turns on you with a grin:

> Pone me pigris ubi nulla campis
> arbor aestiva recreatur aura,
> quod latus mundi nebulae malusque
>   Juppiter urget;
> pone sub curru nimium propinqui
> solis in terra domibus negata:
> dulce ridentem Lalagen amabo,
>   dulce loquentem.

> Put me in barren steppes where not a tree
> Is revived by summer's breeze, in regions
> Of the world, where fogs and
>   angry sky prevail;
> Put me under the sun's chariot when
> Too close to earth, in lands to men forbid,
> Still I shall love my sweetly laughing,
>   Sweetly prattling Lalage.

This is Horace in his gay delightful mood, the Horace known to his friends; no wonder that they, no wonder that Lalage, loved him. The words fit together like precious stones in a goldsmith's ornament, almost like flashing colors dabbed by the

hummingbird brush of Hubert van Eyck. Latin is a masculine
language, fashioned for the use of imperator on the battlefield
and of the praetor in his tribunal, and to see it all tricked out in
feminine grace reveals Horace's exquisite skill.

I cite *Integer vitae* to show the poet's grace and humor. To
illustrate his tenderness I will now cite the twenty-fourth ode in
Book I: the requiem on the death of Quintilius, Horace and
Virgil's friend.

> Quis desiderio sit pudor aut modus
> tam cari capitis? praecipe lugubres
> cantus, Melpomene, cui liquidam pater
>   vocem cum cithara dedit.
>
> ergo Quintilium perpetuus sopor
> urget? cui Pudor et Justitiae soror,
> incorrupta Fides, nudaque Veritas,
>   quando ullum inveniet parem?
>
> multis ille bonis flebilis occidit,
> nulli flebilior quam tibi, Vergili.
> tu frustra pius heu non ita creditum
>   poscis Quintilium deos.
>
> quid, si Threicio blandius Orpheo
> auditam moderere arboribus fidem?
> num vanae redeat sanguis imagini,
>   quam virga semel horrida,
>
> non lenis precibus fata recludere,
> nigro compulerit Mercurius gregi?
> durum: sed levius fit patientia,
>   quicquid corrigere est nefas.

What restraint or limit can there be to grief for so dear a life? O you,
Melpomene, to whom our Father Jupiter gave the lyre and a soft sweet
voice, teach me a song of sorrow!

Does, indeed, everlasting sleep press Quintilius down? When shall Modesty, and Justice's sister, incorruptible Honor, and naked Truth, e'er find

his equal? Many good men weep his death, none shall shed more tears than you, Virgil. In vain, virtuous though you are, you ask the Gods to give Quintilius back — he was not lent to us, alas, upon such terms.

What, if you should play more winningly than Thracian Orpheus upon the lyre, that trees once listened to ? Will life return to the incorporeal ghost, which Mercury, ungentle to break down Fate for prayers, has once with horrid wand driven among the shadowy flock? It is hard. But that which would be sacrilege to change, patience makes easier to bear.

What more can mortal say when death knocks at the heart of a friend? What can consolation do but praise the dead, share another friend's grief, and bid him summon up his courage to bear with patience what must be borne? And how harmonious and tender some lines are:

> nulli flebilior quam tibi, Vergili,

or,

> quid, si Threicio blandius Orpheo.

I think that no other odes give so true a glimpse into Horace's nature as do these two.

But he was versatile, he could write lyrically and charmingly, as he does in Odes III, IX, which I call *A Lover's Quarrel* (I quote the Bennett translation.)

While I was dear to thee and no more favoured youth flung his arms about thy dazzling neck, I lived in greater bliss than Persia's king.

While thou wast enamoured of no other more than me, and Lydia ranked not after Chloë, in joy of my great fame I, Lydia, lived more glorious than Roman Ilia.

Me Thracian Chloë now doth sway, skilled in sweet measures and mistress of the lyre; for her I will not fear to die, if the Fates but spare my darling and suffer her to live.

Me Calais, son of Thurian Ornytus, kindles with mutual flame; for him right willingly I twice will die, if the Fates but spare the lad and suffer him to live.

What if the old love come back again and join those now estranged beneath her compelling yoke; if fair-haired Chloë be put aside and the door thrown open to rejected Lydia?

Though he is fairer than the stars, and thou less stable than the tossing cork and stormier than the wanton Adriatic, with thee I fain would live, with thee I'd gladly die.

This is charming, and seems to belong to some other country and some other age (so touched it is with half-real, half-artificial, gallantry), Herrick, or Lovelace, Pope perhaps, or Austin Dobson, might have written it. There are other poems that belong to the same mood: the odes to Venus (Odes I, xxx), and to Diana (Odes III, xxi) — pretty verses, composed for pleasure, perhaps at the instance of Leuconoë or Lalage, perhaps to grace a company of guests.

I speak of these as artificial poems. But all of Horace's poems are artificial, for they are all the product of premeditation — of consummate art, of deliberation, of labor long slept upon. He never felt the dithyrambic power of inspiration. One, however, and that one of his most famous poems, seems to me as near spontaneity as his artistic conscience would permit. I mean the ode on the *Fons Bandusiae* (Odes III, xiii), the spring to which I have referred, that has given many a scholar pilgrim the comfortable satisfaction that he has at last discovered the *Fons* that none of his predecessors, in spite of their zeal, in spite of their certainty, had ever hit upon. However that may be, the dazzling fountain of itself is but a happy concentration of water drops bursting from a hidden recess dug by nature in the material earth; the soul of the *Fons Bandusiae*, its Genius, its nymph, lives in Horace's poem:

O Fons Bandusiae, splendidior vitro,
dulci digne mero non sine floribus,
  cras donaberis haedo,
    cui frons turgida cornibus

primis et venerem et proelia destinat,
frustra: nam gelidos inficiet tibi
rubro sanguine rivos
lascivi suboles gregis.

te flagrantis atrox hora Caniculae
nescit tangere, tu frigus amabile
fessis vomere tauris
praebes et pecori vago.

fies nobilium tu quoque fontium,
me dicente cavis impositam ilicem
saxis, unde loquaces
lymphae desiliunt tuae.

O Fountain of Bandusia, more resplendent than crystal, worthy of flowers and sweet wine, tomorrow you shall receive a kid, whose forehead with swelling horns portends love and battles, in vain. This offspring of the wanton herd shall color your cold waters with its crimson blood. You, the cruel season of the burning Dog Star cannot touch. You, to bullocks weary of the plow and to wandering sheep, offer grateful coolness. And you among famous fountains shall be, because it is I that sing of the oak growing over the hollow rock from which your babbling waters leap.

You cannot guess from this jejune prose what a delicate work of art the poem is. But you do learn that honors are to be paid to the fountain, and of the charitable deeds that caused those honors, and finally that the fountain is to receive a further reward even greater than the sacrifice of a kid — and here creeps in the same little ironical smile that was manifest in *Integer vitae — me dicente . . . impositam ilicem!*" because I sing of the oak tree!"

The meter is called the Fourth Asclepiadean. There was a Greek poet of Samos, a friend of Theocritus, who gave his name to several meters, of which this is one. It was well chosen for a poem on a fountain. The dactyls, two in the first line (one in

the first half, one in the second), another in the third line, and
another in the fourth, give an intermittent light, leaping, frolic
suggestion of flowing water, that iambic or trochaic verse could
not do. And, examining with care, and perhaps imagination, the
reader discovers other little touches that call bubbling waters to
mind: the combinations *floribus* and *cornibus, fessis . . . tauris,
impositam ilicem, nobilium . . . fontium,* and the alliteration
rubro rivos. And I think, or imagine, that one detects a special
use of vowels, which Horace chose by ear, and not as I have done
by count. For example, in *Fons Bandusiae* there are 44 i's, most
of them short, 26 o's, most of them broad, as against 19 a's and
16 u's. And note the three *ili's* in the last stanza of the ode just
quoted; the rush and gush of the fountain kept echoing in his
ears and he sought to convey the sounds to his readers.

But what I am coming to is that Horace is able to take the
stately Latin idiom — fit language for lawgivers, for imperators
and orators, for a description of the Gallic War or a denunciation
of Catiline — and use it almost onomatopoetically to describe a
fountain. Read over the last stanza and mark how felicitously
successful he has been in the choice and arrangement of words.
You understand why Petronius used the phrase *curiosa felicitas*
in praising Horace. The medium was recalcitrant, and to show
how much so, I will quote from the derivative poem *La Fontaine Bellerie* by Ronsard.

> Tu es la Nymphe eternelle
> De ma terre paternelle:
> Pource en ce pré verdelet
> Voy ton Poëte qui t'orne
> D'un petit chevreau de lait,
> A qui l'une et l'autre corne
> Sortent du front nouvelet.

L'ardeur de la Canicule
   Ton verd rivage ne brule,
   Tellement qu'en toutes pars
   Ton ombre est espaisse et druë
   Aux pasteurs venans des parcs,
   Aux bœufs las de la charruë,
   Et au bestial espars.

Iô! tu seras sans cesse
   Des fontaines la princesse,
   Moy celebrant le conduit
   Du rocher percé, qui darde
   Avec un enroué bruit
   L'eau de ta source jazarde
   Qui trepillante se suit.

Here we have a language, fresh from the court of François Premier, gay, gallant, merry, full of hope and confidence that all is well with the world, carefree and charming. The poem is the very nymph of the fountain, swaying, dancing, swirling, scattering drops like kisses to the flowers on her banks. The difference between the two poems is partly that between the two languages, but also that between the Augustan Age and the High Renaissance. I have quoted it so fully because it enables one to see how hard it must have been for Horace to soften and limber the rugged Latin language into so delicate a form, and to create so charming a chef-d'œuvre.

There are other odes; the first six in Book III have had a great and special interest attached to them. Personally I think their importance has been undeservedly exaggerated, but they have received so much attention from editors and commentators that out of a decent regard for distinguished scholars, I shall return to them, following, as I think I should, a circuitous way.

XVII

HORACE AND AUGUSTUS

THE Emperor was away from Rome from early in 31 B.C. till August 29 B.C., during which time Horace published the second book of Satires and the Epodes. The scant references to Caesar (as he was usually called before he assumed the title Augustus) in these two works suggest that the poet had at that time little personal acquaintance with him. In fact, in Satire 1, Book II, when it is suggested that Horace write of Caesar the poet replies: "I shall not fail myself when occasion serves. Except at just the right moment Caesar's ears will not be open, and Flaccus' words will find no admittance. Stroke him awkwardly, and he is on his guard and kicks out on every side." This certainly seems to show that, though it was likely that as a friend of Maecenas Horace was known to Caesar, the acquaintance stopped there.

After the victory at Actium came the great work of organizing the Empire. Opportunity for intimacy was scant. The Emperor needed leisure before he could interest himself in literary matters and seek out the farmer poet. Horace, too, had to go half-way. The youthful republican, when he came back to Rome from Philippi, must have been reluctant to turn his opinions inside out, to seem, if only to himself, a renegade. Then he came under the influence of Maecenas, who strongly believed that the old Republican system was outworn, inapplicable to the Roman world, and must be superseded by an imperial government. And under Augustus life became easier and easier for private citizens such as Horace: he grew more attached to his Sabine farm and his lazy life — talking matters over with his bailiff, pottering in his garden, pretending that he knew about the gentle art of grafting, ordering foreign wines as well as superintending the vintage of his own Sabine grapes. Gradually the comforts of peace, or order, and of law, like the summer sun on snow, melted away Horace's rugged republican ideas.

Once Horace clearly understood what immense benefits Augustus' policy conferred upon the people, his admiration of the Emperor grew and grew. In ode after ode he chaunts the Emperor's accomplishments. He hails him, long before the senate followed his lead, as *Pater et Princeps;* he rates him second only to Jupiter; he says he shall sip nectar with the gods, that he is ministered to by the Muses, and declares that Romans need not fear civil strife or death by violence while Caesar reigns (Odes I, ii; I, xii; III, iii; III, iv; III, xiv; III, xxv).

In the Odes you come upon a cheerful note of happy confidence in the present and the future. How different from the generations before. One has to read Cicero's letter to appreciate this note in its fullness. Poor Cicero with the black background of rivalry and war between Julius Caesar and Pompey, and after the fatal Ides of March, the dark figure of Mark Antony! But for Horace, with Caesar Augustus on the throne, the storm is over and gone and turtle-doves coo in the Sabine elms.

The twenty-ninth ode in Book I expresses this note of confidence to which I have referred. One of Horace's friends, Iccius, a studious cultivated man, interested in philosophy, proposes to join an expedition of conquest into Arabia and Horace rallies him on the foolish project.

Iccius, do you really covet the rich treasures of the Arabians? Are you preparing to make war on those Sabaean kings, who have never yet been conquered? Are you forging chains for the horrible Medes? What barbarian maiden is to become your slave, after you have slain her lover? What page from the royal palace, with perfumed hair, is to be your cup-bearer? Who will now assert that rivers can not flow backward up the hills, and the Tiber reverse its course, when you, of whom we expected better things, are set on exchanging Socratic philosophy and the noble books of Panaetius for a Spanish breast-plate?

It would be hard to express a sense of security more forcibly. Horace will not take the notion of war seriously. The *Pax Romana* is built on a rock, and going off to Arabia to fight is fantastic. What monstrous conduct, what idiocy, to abandon philosophy for a soldier's life! It would have been impossible for a poet to have written in such a strain before the overthrow of Antony and Cleopatra, before Augustus Caesar had transformed the world. But now, for Horace, the Sabine farm, old Falernian, a picnic by the banks of the Digentia constitute the realities; war and its attendant robberies are merely such stuff as bad dreams are made of.

The ode to Sestius (Odes I, iv) is another reflection of Augustus' government, and tells the same tale of peace and content. Bitter winter melts away to make place for Favonius and Spring. The meadows are no longer white with hoar frost, Venus leads forth her dancing troop, Graces and Nymphs trip it on the light fantastic toe. Now it is meet to deck our heads with flowers and sacrifice a kid to Faunus.

Surely this suggests the inauguration of a new Golden Age. Even the solemn note near the end carries on the same idea,

> pallida Mors aequo pulsat pede pauperum tabernas
> regumque turres.

> Pale death with impartial foot knocks at the
> Poor man's hut and at the royal palace.

for it is an allegation that all that Romans need fear is natural death, never more assassination, civil swords, or foreign spears.

I press this point, for I wish to make it clear that Horace did not drop his republican creed and acquiesce to the monarchy merely from selfish, personal reasons, but because all circumstances cried aloud that the reign of Augustus was a universal blessing.

With the publication of the first three books of Odes Horace was one of the first men in Rome, the foremost poet while Virgil was away, a boon companion of Maecenas, a friend of Agrippa, Pollio, Plancus, and gradually as the years passed of the great Emperor Augustus. The Emperor was kindly disposed towards him, credulous no doubt of Maecenas' praises. But an absolute ruler, no matter how much he condescends, cannot meet other men in the genial warmth of a common humanity. But — perhaps as a consequence of the praises of Augustus in the Odes, perhaps by a twist of circumstance — from the time the Odes were published the relations between the two men became more intimate.

This intimacy is well illustrated by Augustus' letters (quoted from Rolfe's edition of Suetonius), for example this one to Horace:

Onysius has brought me your little book, which though it is very small, I accept in good part, as bringing its own apology. Apparently you are afraid lest your books may be bigger than yourself. But though you lack stature, you do not lack girth. It would be a good idea to write on a pint pot, so the rotundity of your volume may resemble that of your belly.

And sometime, at a later date one may suppose, Augustus offered Horace the post of private secretary, for he writes to Maecenas:

Up till now I have been strong enough to write letters myself to my personal friends. But now I am terribly busy and not very well, and therefore I should like to filch from you your friend Horace. So please let him come from that eleemosynary table of yours to my table in the palace, and help me in writing letters.

Horace refused. There was nothing that he would have liked less, and Augustus took the refusal in good part. Another scrap out of a letter from Augustus to Horace is proof that the refusal made no difference whatever in their relations: "Please make yourself entirely at home in my house, as if you were a member of the household. That will be quite correct, for I wanted us to be on that footing, if your health had permitted it."

XVIII

THE DIDACTIC ODES

OCTAVIUS returned to Rome in 29 B.C. to be greeted as a savior. *Roma conservata* held out her arms to him. The day of his birth, the day of Actium, and the day of his entry into Alexandria were named sacred. Triumphs were awarded him, and his name was inserted among those of the Gods in ceremonial hymns. He was called *Princeps,* and the senate, on the proposal of Horace's friend Plancus, bestowed upon him the title Augustus which carried with it an almost religious implication.

The great matter to be accomplished was the constitution of the Roman state. The historian Dio Cassius reports at length the counsels that Maecenas and Agrippa gave Augustus. Those of Maecenas prevailed. The state was reorganized on a monarchial basis. The Emperor held the real power, though it was cloaked in traditional republican forms. Augustus, in the account inscribed on the tablets discovered in Ancyra, says: "I declined to accept any office inconsistent with the institutions of our ancestors. . . . I stood above all others in authority but of actual power I possessed no more than my colleagues in each separate magistracy." It is plain, however, that in spite of specious powers conferred upon the senate, Augustus was in fact an autocrat. But Strabo, a contemporary says: "Never had Rome and her allies enjoyed richer blessings of peace and prosperity than those which Augustus bestowed upon them."

The constitution was the first concern. Next came the material building and rebuilding of imperial Rome: the temples of Vesta, Jupiter Capitolinus, Mars Ultor, and Apollo on the Palatine, the Julian Mausoleum, and so forth. Encouraged by the Emperor, Agrippa completed the Saepta Julia and erected the Pantheon; Statilius Taurus built an amphitheatre and Plancus a temple to Saturn. At the end Augustus was able to say that he had found the city brick, but left it marble.

But Augustus had other plans and dreams for the Roman people, more important than architecture and politics — plans and dreams to restore the old Roman character. John Buchan says: "Augustus desired for Rome . . . not only political reform but a moral and religious regeneration."

He suppressed crime, he alleviated the lot of slaves, he condemned adultery, he was just and merciful. Furthermore, whether he agreed with Ovid that "the existence of Gods is expedient, and it is expedient that we should believe in their existence" and acted from political motives, or whether from actual religious convictions, he restored the ancient temples and fostered the ancient beliefs of the common people. He strove to restore the old Roman *pietas* and *gravitas*, the principles of Regulus, Marcellus, Cato Major, and others niched in the Roman Hall of Fame. He himself said: "I restored to honor the examples of our forefathers which were disappearing from our manners and I have myself left examples worthy of being imitated by my descendants."

I cannot do better with regard to the achievements of Augustus than to quote the historian Velleius Paterculus:

As for Caesar's return to Italy and to Rome — the procession which met him, the enthusiasm of his reception by men of all classes, ages, and ranks, and the magnificence of his triumphs and of the spectacles which he gave — all this would be impossible adequately to describe. . . . There is nothing that man can desire from the gods, nothing that the gods can grant to a man, nothing that wish can conceive or good fortune bring to pass, which Augustus on his return to the city did not bestow upon the republic, the Roman people, and the world. The civil wars were ended after twenty years, foreign wars suppressed, peace restored, the frenzy of arms everywhere lulled to rest; validity was restored to the laws, authority to the courts, and dignity to the senate; the power of the magistrates was reduced to its former limits. . . . The old traditional form of the republic was restored. Agriculture returned to the fields, respect to religion, to mankind freedom from anxiety, and to each citizen his property rights were now assured; old laws were usefully amended, and new laws passed for the general good.

There can be no doubt that Horace looked upon Augustus' achievements with the same eyes as Velleius Paterculus. He was stirred by the Emperor's noble ambitions, more stirred than he had been since he was swept off his feet by republican fervor at the time when Brutus arrived in Athens. He loved his country, he was proud of being a Roman, that thought brought him more than comfort, it brought to him a sense of obligation. He had received, he must give back. He was a poet, and he could aid the Emperor's admirable efforts by writing verses. It was quite unnecessary to suppose that Maecenas or anybody else besought his help. Horace wanted to do all he could for Rome, for his fellow Romans, so he wrote the celebrated six odes which he placed at the beginning of Book III.

He took great pains in the composition, but not, in my judgment, with the same success as in other odes more suitable to his habitual epicurean mode of thought. I sometimes wonder if a little ironical smile flitted over his lips, to think of himself, with his panoply of skepticisms, working at the moral and religious rehabilitation of the Roman people. Nevertheless, his heart was in his work, and his patriotism gives an heroic enlargement to the stature of that little man, otherwise so independent, so ironical, so gentle, so genial, so lazy, and so delightful.

These six odes, all in the Alcaic meter, are certainly connected in spirit, and most scholars give them a position apart from the general text. But those commentators who speak as if Horace, through these odes, had become a sort of co-builder of empire with Augustus, are surely misled by their enthusiasm. Although Horace repeatedly sets forth the Augustan ideals, there is also an occasional note of pessimism, and throughout the odes runs a strong strain of disdain and contempt for the masses — writing not calculated to rally the common people to an autocratic emperor who wished his government to rest upon their support. To indicate what I mean, I will make a cursory examination of the odes.

Ode 1 begins:

> Odi profanum vulgus et arceo;
> favete linguis. carmina non prius
>   audita Musarum sacerdos
>   virginibus puerisque canto,

> I hate the profane crowd and keep it away;
> Please be quiet. I, a priest of the Muses,
>   Sing to maids and boys songs
>   Never before heard,

and continues: Kings rule over their subjects, Jupiter rules over kings. One man is richer, better born, more successful than another. Impartial fate determines each man's lot. He over whose head the sword of Damocles hangs, cares not for feasts, nor will music bring him slumber. Sweet sleep comes to the poor man. He that only desires enough, need not be afraid of stormy seas,

nor hail, nor rain, nor heat, nor snow. The rich man is dogged
by fear, black care sits on the knight's crupper. Luxury cannot
soothe distress, why should I build a palace, or exchange my
Sabine farm for burdensome riches?

Good verses and well composed, and wholly in harmony with
Augustus' work of moral rehabilitation, but do they wipe out the
aristocratic disdain of the opening stanza?

Ode II runs:

> Angustam amice pauperiem pati
> robustus acri militia puer
> condiscat.

Let youth, robust from military discipline, learn to accept kindly
the pinch of poverty. Let it live out-of-doors amid stirring deeds.
Dulce et decorum est pro patria mori. True manhood never
knows ignoble defeat. *Sans peur et reproche*, it neither takes nor
lays down office at the behest of popular favor. True manhood
scorns the common crowd and flies away from muddy earth.

This is fired with patriotism and extols hardihood, but is it
the language to win the common people? It sounds more like
Coriolanus, the haughty aristocrat. I stress the point that Horace
agrees heart and soul with Augustus in his program of moral
and religious regeneration, but that he does not go along with
him in his treatment of Demos. Julius Caesar had courted the
plebs, and Augustus had followed his example. Horace was
generous-minded, but he was by nature of aristocratical bent. He
had always scorned the multitude "which in its folly elects the
unworthy to office and is stupidly subservient to notoriety," and
speaks of himself as "far, far removed from them" (Sat. I, vi).

Ode III continues the praise of steadfastness:

> Justum et tenacem propositi virum
> non civium ardor prava jubentium,

> non vultus instantis tyranni
> mente quatit solida,

> The righteous man tenacious of his purpose
> Is not shaken in his fixed resolutions
> By the fury of his fellow citizens
> Bidding him do wrong,
> Nor by the looks of the threatening tyrant,

and later includes a solemn warning not to come to terms with Asia and the East; but those words *civium ardor prava jubentium* display the same Coriolanus-like contempt for the masses that was surely contrary to the Emperor's policy.

Ode IV treats of the defense of the Titans by the gods, an allegory to extol the victory at Actium. But the citizens of Rome were so obviously delighted by the defeat of Antony and the restoration of law and order that the lesson was scarcely needed.

Ode V praises Augustus and his works:

> Caelo tonantem credidimus Jovem
> regnare;

> We believe that Jupiter reigns in heaven,
> Because we hear his thunderbolt.

Augustus shall be deemed a God among us for annexing the Britons and Persians to our empire. Crassus' soldiers surrendered, married barbarian wives, and lived subject to a Persian king, forgetful of Rome — O shame! How different Regulus, who was released from his Carthaginian captivity for the purpose of persuading the Roman Senate to accept the Carthaginian terms. He went, but bade the Romans reject the treaty, and then returned to Carthage, as to his home, to be tortured as he well knew, and killed.

Here Horace indisputably supports Augustus' purpose "to re-

store to honor the examples of our forefathers," but to praise
Regulus, one of the greatest national heroes, was hardly enough
to make him a collaborator with the Emperor in the restoration
of Rome.

Ode VI supports Augustus' plan for religious rehabilitation:

> Delicta majorum immeritus lues,
> Romane, donec templa refeceris
>   aedesque labentes deorum et
>   foeda nigro simulacra fumo.

> Thou shall pay for thy fathers' sins
> O Roman, though guiltless, until
>   Thou shalt restore the falling temples of the Gods
>   And their statues black with smoke.

Lack of religion is the cause of all evil. Our times are sinful.
Our maidens learn Ionian dances, then coquetry, then adultery,
while the husbands connive. Not born of such parents were the
soldiers who beat back Pyrrhus and Antiochus and Hannibal, but
of sturdy country folk.

    But the last stanza says,

> What does not time, the spoiler, render less?
> The age of our parents was inferior to that
> Of our grandparents, ours is worse,
> And our children shall be more wicked still.

This ode does not sound the note of hope, not at all. It draws a
gloomy picture of the present, and augurs ill for the future.
How does this uphold the Emperor's policy?

    At any rate, I have given you examples of what has been con-
sidered to be Horace's contribution to the reëdification of the
Roman state. His preaching — I suppose it should be regarded

as preaching — is, for the most part, done with consideration and delicacy. Softened and sweetened by a dextrous arrangement of ideas, he commends moderation, frugality, simplicity, hardihood, training of the body, discipline of the spirit, steadfastness, love of justice, and patriotism, and he denounces oriental luxury with its attendants, effeminacy and vice. This is much. But I think that Horace wrote from a desire to express the thoughts that arose in his heart as he watched what Augustus was striving for, rather than from any conscious purpose of co-building the Empire with the Emperor.

XIX

EPISTLES, BOOK I

AFTER the completion of the three books of Odes, Horace turned to a fourth poetical form. He had begun with satires, proceeded to epodes, on to odes, and now composed epistles in verse. The first epistle explains the reason for this change in form, but perhaps there was also an element of laziness in the shift, for lyrical poems are hard work. The Greek meters are complicated and exacting, but the epistles are in familiar hexameters. The epistolary form had a double value in his eyes, it enabled him to preach and it almost compelled him to talk of himself. Like that other little man of great wit and independent mind, Michel de Montaigne, and like almost all other men, Horace enjoyed talking about himself. And the form brought the satisfaction of change, of novelty, besides enabling him to say what he wanted in the way he wanted to say it. He had attained, he felt, enduring fame as a poet and now he would please himself, he would sit in his curule chair, and moralize, admonish, blame, praise, say what he liked, and per-

haps what others too would like. Epistles would be his sermons
and at the same time he could say, "C'est moi que je peins."

In his opening epistle to Maecenas he says that he has grown
older, that it is time to abandon lyrical poems and other frivoli-
ties and cultivate philosophy — *quid verum atque decens curo et
rogo et omnis in hoc sum,* "whatever is true and of good report I
value and pursue, that is my only interest." He says that he belongs to no school of philosophy, a statement quite consistent
with membership in the Epicurean sect, for the Epicureans
lightly cross the low fence that bounds their garden, and pick
what flowers and fruits may grow outside. *Quo me cumque
rapit tempestas, deferor hospes,* "wherever the wild wind takes
me I put in and accept the harbor's hospitality." In other words,
he says (in substance): "I climb over the garden fence, where it
is most readily superable, whether into the enclosure of the
Stoics, or the curtilage of the Cyrenaics who teach that pleasure
is our goal, and I hope to find remedies for all my faults." In
saying that he belongs to no one school, he means that he is no
formal philosopher. He says that Homer is a better teacher of
ethics than professors of philosophy are, whatever the sect, and
bids us imitate Ulysses and dare follow wisdom, *sapere aude,*
and spurn delight, *sperne voluptates.* "He that does not curb
his anger will wish what he has done were undone and what he
has said unsaid."

He sets forth his ideas in bits, scraps, fragments. He is full of
maxims, which is often a happy way of both talking of himself,
of his likes, his creed, and at the same time of admonishing his
hearers; thus he writes in the first epistle:

> Virtus est vitium fugere et sapientia prima
> stultitia caruisse.

Virtue is to flee from vice and the beginning of wisdom is to be
free from folly. Beware the lust of money! The Portico of

Janus [Wall Street] cries out: "Hear ye, hear ye! The first thing to aim at is money, virtue comes after money. Get money, honestly if you can, but anyhow get money."

Then the poet asks, "Are such counsellors wiser than he who bids you stand erect and free, and defy fortune?"

Horace's maxims savor of Ben Franklin and also of Polonius. They are always in support of virtue, but usually along a high-road of well-trodden thoughts, where the interest lies not so much in the value of the maxims as in the simple hospitable way they are set before us. And always there is the pleasure of meeting Horace's personality.

The more personal epistles I find the most sympathetic. Many of Horace's letters were to young soldiers. It was the custom of young Roman gentlemen of prominent families to join the staff of a distinguished general, and make a campaign or two under his leadership, in order to learn the practice of war, to see strange lands, and acquire worldly experience away from home. The experience they gained would always be useful, though they might not mean to become professional soldiers, and the fashion drew young men even when without martial mettle.

These letters tell us more than any historian about the position Horace occupied in Rome. He was now past forty, and his arms and legs and his back were less ready to dig sods and roll away stones than they had been, and he must have passed a good deal of time in the city, for these young men of fashion would hardly be leaving the dissipations that Rome bountifully afforded, for a stay in the Sabine Hills. They all made a fad of poetry. It had long been the mode for young patricians to worship the Muses as well as Mars, and the tradition held fast. Cicero and Julius Caesar, wrote verses, as did Quintus Cicero, Augustus, Mark Antony's son, Pollio, Gallus, and many others. And these young men of Tiberius' generation no doubt took their verses seriously. Horace was their oracle. They clustered about him as the chief priest of the Muses, laid their productions before him, discussed principles and particulars, criticised the living and the dead, asked his advice, with the ultimate consequence, as we shall see, that for their benefit he wrote long literary essays in verse, to expound his opinions.

Horace knew a number of young Roman gentlemen, — Celsus Albinovanus, Titius, Munatius, Julius Florus — who accompanied Tiberius, the Emperor's stepson, on his campaign to Armenia, where he was sent to place the Roman candidate, Tigranes, upon the throne (20 B.C.). Tiberius was young and a cultivated man and liked to have about him young men who were interested in Greek poetry and Greek mythology. Horace had a great liking for these young men, as his epistle to Julius Florus shows (Epis. I, III):

Dear Julius Florus, I am struggling to find out in what regions of the earth Tiberius is now campaigning. Are you in Thrace, does frozen Hebrus stop you, are you in the province of Asia? And what is that *studiosa cohors*, that learned staff, composing? Which of you is celebrating the exploits of Augustus? Is Titius imitating Pindar, or is he writing tragedies? Is Celsus learning to express himself, and not to copy other poets? And what are you venturing on? *Quae circumvolitas agilis thyma?* What beds of thyme are your quick wings hovering about? If you could but leave your ambitions behind, you would journey there where heavenly wisdom would lead. That is the task for us to speed, great and lowly alike, if we wish to be of value to ourselves and of value to our country.

You must also tell me, when you write, how you are getting on with Munatius. Or does your broken friendship, like a wound ill sewn, close without healing and tear open again? It is unworthy of you both to break the bond of brotherhood — wild untamed creatures. But whether hot blood or ignorance of correct conduct drives you on and in whatever part of the world you are living, a heifer ready for the sacrifice is feeding fat against your return.

There is also an epistle (Epis. I, VIII) to another of these young men on the staff of Tiberius, Celsus Albinovanus, which I have quoted in part before:

Dear Muse, I ask you please to tell Celsus Albinovanus, secretary and companion of Tiberius, that I hope he is happy and prosperous. If he asks you how I am, tell him that in spite of my fine boastings, I am neither living nobly nor very agreeably. It is not because hail has beaten down my vines, nor because the heat has blighted my olives, nor that my cattle are sick in my far flung fields, but because my mind is less well than any part of my body. I don't want to listen to anything or learn anything that will cure my sickness. I am rude to my faithful physicians, I get angry with my friends and ask them why they make such an ado to keep me from a fatal lethargy. I continue to pursue what has been bad for me and run from what I believe would do me good. I am wayward as the wind; at Rome I long for Tibur, at Tibur I long for Rome.

After this (dear Muse) ask Celsus how he is, how his affairs and he are getting on, how he stands with the young prince and his staff. If he says, "Very well," first congratulate him, and then remember to drop this precept in his ear, "As you bear your good fortune, Celsus, so shall we bear you."

This letter appears to be a carefully considered and ingeniously composed warning to his young friend not to let good fortune turn his head.

More interesting to lovers of poetry is the epistle to Albius Tibullus (Epis. I, IV), the young sentimental, melancholy poet. Poor Tibullus had been treated ill by a girl he loved — perhaps these verses of his had reached Horace's ears:

Rumor ait crebro nostram peccare puellam.

Rumor says my girl is often unfaithful. I could wish my ears were deaf. I suffer when such things are said. Cruel Rumor, why do you torture your victim so. Be silent.

"O! Beware my lord, of jealousy." Horace, himself, had felt, in a mild way touches of it, and he wrote an ode of condolence to his friend (Odes I, xxxiii). Now perhaps he suspected that Tibullus was again in need of cheer, a change of thought and a little flattery, always the best of medicines.

Albius, candid critic of my satires, what am I to understand that you are doing in the country at Pedum? Writing something that will outdo the poems by Cassius of Parma, or wandering silent in the health-giving woods, musing on all that is worthy of a good man and wise? You were never a body without a soul. The gods gave you beauty, the gods gave you riches, and the art of enjoyment. You think aright, and you are able to express what you feel, you have health and fame and charm in full measure, a goodly living, a never failing purse — what more would a nurse pray for her sweet child?

Nevertheless amid hopes and cares, amid fears and bouts of anger, expect each day that dawns to be your last. Every hour unhoped for will come the more welcome. As for me, when you want to laugh, you will find me fat, shining, my skin well cared for, a pig from Epicurus' herd.

There is another epistle that is, in a way, connected with the letters to the young men on campaign, for it is addressed to Tiberius himself (Epis. I, ix). Tiberius is an enigmatic figure, ill spoken of by Suetonius and Tacitus. But Horace, who knew the Emperor in his youth, calls him *bonus clarusque*, "good and great"; and Velleius Paterculus, who served under him says: "Nurtured by the teachings of eminent preceptors, a youth equipped to the highest degree with the advantages of birth, personal beauty, commanding presence, and excellent education combined with native talents, Tiberius gave early promise of becoming the great man he is now." (I quote the Shipley translation.)

This epistle from Horace was written when the prince was a tall, strong, and handsome young man of twenty-two, already an able soldier. He was a good Greek scholar, spoke the language readily, and composed Greek verses in imitation of poets of the late Alexandrian school, elaborate, didactic, artificial to a high degree. Horace evidently admired him. This epistle reveals on what familiar terms Horace was with Tiberius, and therefore with Augustus, for Horace's friendship for Tiberius must have been a consequence of his intimacy with the Emperor. Incidentally, Addison highly commended this letter.

Septimius is the only man, I'm sure, who knows how much you make of me! For when he asks and (can you believe it?) by his supplications compels me to praise him to you, and recommend him as worthy of the mind of a Nero (patron of all things honorable) and of a place in your household, on the theory that I enjoy a position of greater intimacy — he sees and knows the extent of what power I have, much better than I do.

I said a great deal to him to explain why I should be excused from this action. But I was afraid lest I be thought to be concealing the extent of my influence and pretending it to be less than it is, in order to keep it for my own benefit. So, for the sake of avoiding the shame of a greater fault, I have stooped to claim the privileges of town-bred impudence. And if you approve of my laying modesty aside at the bidding of a friend, please admit Septimius to your circle and believe him to be brave and good.

Finally, I will quote one other epistle, this one to Maecenas:

I admit it. I promised you I should stay only a week in the country, but I have broken my promise. I have stayed away the whole of August, nevertheless, Maecenas, now that I am fearful of falling ill again, and early figs and the heat are calling out the undertaker and his black-robed attendants, if you wish me to be well and strong, you must grant me the same indulgence that you did when I was ill. This is the time when fond fathers and mothers are pale with fear for their children, when social duties and business details bring on fevers and lead to the reading of wills.

However, if the winter shall cover the Alban fields with snow, your poet will go to the seaside, and coddle himself. He will huddle up and read books. And when the breath of spring and the swallows come, sweet friend, he will if you permit, go to visit you. . . . If you will never let me leave you, you must give me back sound lungs, and black locks on my forehead, you must give me back my power of jolly talk and light-hearted laughter, and my indignation at saucy Cinara's sudden escape while we were drinking.

In the eyes, or ears, of a Latin scholar there is something very unseemly, almost indecent, in presenting these epistles in this ragged garb. The verse is necessary to show you their Horatian quality. I have given you roughly the words of his mouth, but his verse gives the little twists of his lips, his smile, the light in his eyes, and the tone of his voice. That I cannot give. But you do get, I hope, enough to believe me when I tell you that these epistles are friendly, familiar letters plentifully supplied with gaiety, kindness, good sense, wit, and unconcealed affection, and reveal most agreeably why his friends loved him.

XX

THE LITERARY EPISTLES

IN the previous chapter I spoke of Horace's friendship with the young gentlemen of letters who accompanied Prince Tiberius on his campaign in the East; I also drew the inference that out of his conversations with them was hatched the idea of essays in poetry. Two of these essays, which were published together about 19 B.C. as Book II of the Epistles, and a third, which was probably published separately and is now called the *Ars Poetica* or *De Arte Poetica*, our textbooks call the Literary Epistles.

The first of these epistles is addressed to the young officer Julius Florus, whose acquaintance we have already made; next came the epistle to Augustus. These two letters are always coupled together, though the chronological order is reversed — the epistle to Augustus being placed first (out of notions of etiquette such as Dogberry felt, "And write God first, or God defend but God should go before"). The third, which was probably written later, though scholars do not agree, was addressed to the Pisos, a father and sons, who are otherwise wrapped in darkness.

That accomplished and pleasant scholar, J. W. Mackail, calls these epistles "three delightful essays in verse." Delightful is a subjective word that requires a giver and a receiver. The music of a song lies in the ear of the hearer. The scholar's ear attuned to Latin discovers in Latin poems much that a grosser ear does not detect. I am told that to young literary intellectuals modernistic verse gives exquisite delight. In the interpretation of poetry one cannot judge the value of the interpretation unless one knows something of the interpreter. Dear Reader, I was born and bred in Philistia, "O mon pays, soit mes amours toujours!"

Of the three literary epistles, that to Julius Florus is to my mind the easiest to read. Florus was a young man "over fond of poesy" (to adopt an expression of Lord Byron's about a young Bostonian who had come to worship), or perhaps only in danger of becoming so — at any rate he was distinctly scholarly and at some time, later than his campaign with Tiberius I presume, edited several Latin classics: Ennius, Lucilius, Varro, and so on.

I will give you an idea of the contents of this epistle. It begins by letting us know that Florus complained because Horace had not written him a poem. Horace sets forth his excuses:

I told you when you were starting that I was lazy. After Philippi I was beggared and of necessity took to writing verses for a livelihood, but now I am comfortably off and I don't need to write. And besides I am older, years have taken from me mirth, love-making, feasting, games, and now they are engaged in wrenching away my powers of poetry. And, anyhow, what would you have me write? One man likes lyrics, another iambics, a third satire.

Moreover it is impossible to write verses in Rome. There are dozens of obstacles. One man asks me to go on his bond, another to drop what I am doing and listen to his literary compositions. I must go to the Quirinal Hill, to a man there who keeps to his bed and then to the very end of the Aventine! As you know, it is a comfortable walk between. You suggest that the streets are clear and that I can go on composing verses as I walk!

A contractor, with his mules and laborers dashes by, a monstrous crane swings up a stone or a beam, funeral processions butt into ox-carts, a mad dog runs here, a filthy sow runs there. Oh yes, write verses certainly!

And, after all, the poets in Rome constitute a mutual admiration society, and that I don't care for. Besides it is hard work.

> Qui legitimum cupiet fecisse poema,
> cum tabulis animum censoris sumet honesti,

The man that wishes to have composed a poem true to the laws of art will take up, at the same time with his tablets, the spirit of an upright censor. [These lines, as all editors point out, Dr. Johnson used as a motto for his dictionary.] Such a man will remove objectionable words, he will bring out *speciosa vocabula rerum*, picturesque phrases, used by famous writers of old, and also employ new words that have come into general usage. He will aim at strength and clarity, he will prune luxuriant expressions, he will smooth what is rough, and conceal the effort.

The truth is that at any time of life one should leave trifles and become a philosopher, one should no longer go on a search for words to fit into Latin verses, but learn the lilt and melody of life. Covet little. What is the advantage of wealth? The owner of a thing gets only the use of it.

I certainly do not wish for squalid want at home, but, be my ship large or small, I, the passenger, remain the same. Miserliness is a disease. You say you are no miser, well, have all other vices fled from you with miserliness? Is your heart innocent of vain ambition? Are you free from fear of death? Do you laugh at dreams, magic, witches, ghosts? Are you grateful for your birthdays? Do you forgive your friends? Do you grow gentler and better as you grow older?

What good does it do you to pluck out one thorn from many? If you do not know how to live aright, make way for those better fitted. You have played enough, you have eaten and drunk enough; it is time to depart.

The epistle as you see falls into sections: (1) Horace's various excuses for not writing; (2) some good advice to young men of letters; (3) the conviction that at his age a man should leave verses and betake himself to philosophy, care little for money,

correct his faults; and (4) when he has had his fill of the banquet of life, depart satisfied, as Lucretius had advised in a
famous line in *De Rerum Natura:*

> Cur non ut plenus vitae conviva recedis?

And if it seems to us disjointed, wandering from logical sequence, I think we may be sure that Florus and his friends
understood it far better than we do.

The epistle to Augustus was probably written about six years
after the letter to Florus. Suetonius says that the Emperor read
some of Horace's *Sermones* (probably the first book of Epistles),
and seeing that none were addressed to him, wrote to Horace:
"Please let me tell you that I am vexed with you, because in
your numerous writings of this kind you don't address yourself
to me rather than to others. Are you afraid that posterity will
think ill of you, because it will appear that you are a friend of
mine?" And Suetonius adds that, as a consequence, Horace
wrote this epistle.

Professor Tenney Frank says that it is well worth reading.
I bow to his authority. To me it is most worth reading, as evidence of the Emperor's interest in literature. Augustus was eminently a cultivated man, he had considerable proficiency in
Greek, though he could not speak it readily, and he was fairly
acquainted with Greek poetry and had a liking for Greek comedy. In his young days he was very diligent in the study of
elocution, and even on his first campaign against Mark Antony
in Italy when he was scarce twenty, before they had made their
triumvirate, he is said to have read, written, and declaimed
every day.

Later in life he composed a number of discourses in prose
from which he read aloud to his friends, one such was *Rescript
to Brutus respecting Cato*, another *Exhortation to Philosophy,*

and besides these there was an unfinished autobiography. He wrote a poem on Sicily in hexameters, and a book of epigrams. He also began a tragedy, *Ajax*, but was dissatisfied and destroyed it. He thought one should write as one speaks, and he cultivated a clear, simple style, avoiding harsh language and obsolete words. Perspicuity was his object, and for its sake he was ready to sacrifice elegance. He wrote to his granddaughter Agrippina that she must be particularly careful to avoid affectation in writing and speaking. It was on this point that he bantered Maecenas, who was fond of fine phrases, and Tiberius who liked obsolete and far-fetched expressions. He encouraged literature, patronized gifted men of letters, listened "with great patience" to them read their works, whether oratory, poetry, history, or what not. Horace knew these facts, and therefore wrote his epistle on literary matters.

He begins by saying that ancient heroes, Romulus, Bacchus, Castor and Pollux, were not recognized as heroes during their lives, but that today men were setting up altars to the living, to Augustus Caesar, taking oaths in his name, and saying that none like him had ever lived or ever would. This is, one may say, a prodigious compliment, and very dextrously offered, for Horace presents it incidentally as if by this exception to prove the general rule that Romans only appreciated what was old, for in literature, the poet asserts dogmatically, they value only the ancients: Ennius, Naevius, Pacuvius, Accius, Afranius, Plautus. He, however, does not agree that antiquity is proof of merit. He is annoyed to hear a poem found fault with, not because it is inelegant, but because it is modern. He asserts that spite toward the living is the real motive for this preference for the dead. He then makes one of those detours which occur frequently in his poems and refers to the course of Greek civilization and how there was a sudden flowering of all the arts after the Persian wars. He remarks how the Romans, after having devoted themselves for a long time to practical affairs, had now suddenly taken up a craze for scribbling. "Before sunrise, I myself wake up, call for pen, paper, and writing case," and he says it is not a bad thing, for poets have their uses, which he enumerated. From that he goes on to tell of the rude beginnings of Latin poetry, till

Graecia capta ferum victorem cepit,

Greece vanquished, took her fierce victor captive.

It is hard to find any strict sequence of thought in this epistle. Horace's mind flies like a butterfly, tacking, luffing, falling, rising, and yet apparently on its way to reach some goal. He speaks of how the Roman dramatists turned to Sophocles and Aeschylus for models; of comedy, and how Plautus really cared more for money than for art. He speaks of how completely a sensitive playwright is in the hands of his audience, to be blessed or damned, and that he himself would not risk that; he adds that a Roman audience is ignorant, the crowd will interrupt a play in order to see a procession of a conquering soldier — chariots full of spoils, captive kings, and strange animals.

Some poets, however, prefer to have their works read rather than acted, and he begs Caesar to bestow a share of his attention upon them, although he is quite ready to acknowledge their many faults. (It is hard to find logic in the flight of the butterfly.) But after all great heroes require great poets to celebrate them, and he says, "Virgil and Varius, whom you love, justify your judgment and the gifts you have given them to your honor. . . . As for me, I should far rather celebrate your great feats than write my epistles and satires, but I am not able."

This epistle, let me say it bluntly, like a bold Philistine, is only interesting to scholars, persons who know about Latin literature from the time of Livius Andronicus (240 B.C.) and who care what Horace thinks about it.

I shall be still more concise in speaking of the *Epistola ad Pisones,* commonly called *Ars Poetica,* or *De Arte Poetica.* If I felt I needed justification, I could refer you to Goethe, who, I am told, said that no two people would think alike of it, and no single person for ten years together (Wickham, II, 331, note). There is no agreement about when it was written, some say between 24 and 20 B.C., others between 12 and 8 B.C. Nor is anybody sure who the Pisos were. Like the other epistles it is written in hexameter verse. I content myself with quoting from a very brief analysis of the poem made by Professor Fairclough:

(a) A poem demands unity, to be secured by harmony and proportion, as well as a wise choice of subject and good diction. Metre and style must be appropriate to them and to character. A good model will always be found in Homer (lines 1–152).

(b) Dramatic poetry calls for special care — as to character drawing, propriety of representation, length of a play, number of actors, use of the chorus and its music, special features for the satyric type, verse-forms, and employment of Greek models (lines 153–294).

(c) A poet's qualifications include common sense, knowledge of character, adherence to high ideals, combination of the *dulce* with the *utile,* intellectual superiority, appreciation of the noble history and lofty mission of poetry, and above all a willingness to listen to and profit by impartial criticism (lines 295–476).

Even if you were to read the *Ars Poetica* half a dozen times I do not think that you would get a clearer idea of it. But if you are scholarly and have a liking for such matters, read Aristotle's *Poetics,* then this, and then Boileau's *Art Poétique,* and very likely you will be able to give a lucid explanation of Horace's butterfly flights; and to boot you will probably feel very pleased with yourself, a desirable consequence of all human effort.

I should repeat that in this matter I am in the camp of the Philistines, and admit, as I must do, that elsewhere you will find ample encouragement to read all three Literary Epistles, and in especial the *Ars Poetica.* To take a single instance, Sir Theodore Martin says: "The dignity of literature was never better vindicated than in these epistles," and, "The Epistle to the Pisos does not profess to be a complete exposition of the poet's art. . . . So far as it goes, it is all gold, full of most instructive hints for a sound critical taste and a pure literary style." But I may add that in reading the 118 page edition of Sir Theodore's book on Horace I noticed that less than half a page was devoted to the *Ars Poetica.*

The real interest of this literary essay lies in the immense influence it has exercised on the course and criticism of poetry in all Europe.

XXI

LAURIGER HORATIUS

THE Epistles are the product of peace. They bear eloquent testimony to the Emperor's success in restoring order and establishing a reign of law. They concern themselves with peaceful things, with reading Homer, with writing poetry, with precepts on the value of philosophy; on strolling in the woods, on a dinner party, on virtue, and so forth. There is no black shadow of danger round the corner, of death peeping in at the window, of malice domestic. This was what Augustus had accomplished.

By the year 17 B.C. the greatest tasks were behind him. He had adjusted old machinery to new functions, he had adapted old formulas to new needs, he had suppressed revolts in Gaul and Spain, and it seemed to him well to show gratitude to the Gods for their goodness to him and to Rome. He decided to celebrate the *Ludi Saeculares,* a great religious ceremony, handed down by the Fathers, which had been celebrated at about the end of each hundred years. That date, according to an official interpretation of a Sybilline oracle, would fall due in May, and great preparations were made for it.

The chief feature of the ceremony was to be a hymn to Apollo and Diana, sung by a chorus of boys and maidens in the new temple to Apollo in the Palatine. There could be no doubt as to who should compose it. Virgil was dead, young Tibullus also, Propertius and Ovid were much younger, and the choice of Horace as the official poet was a matter of course. It was during the years just before this that the friendship between Augustus and Horace had been growing; nevertheless, not friendship but a recognition of Horace's preëminence caused the selection. The Emperor confirmed what would have been the people's choice. Horace was not merely admired by the intellectuals, but also by the public. As he walked the streets, men said: "That's he, there goes Horace, the poet."

It has been asked whether this appointment gave him any such office as would justify the title poet laureate. Probably not. At least it is usual for scholars to deny him the title. No doubt they are right. He received no pipe of Caecuban wine at Neptune's fete, no haunch of wild boar at the Saturnalia, and yet he performed some of the duties that would fall to a poet laureate, not only in composing the *Carmen Saeculare* but also odes in honor of the Emperor and his two stepsons, Tiberius and Drusus. These were to come later. The *Carmen Saeculare* is his most notable official act.

All preparations for the great festival were ready by the time appointed. On the last day of May, at night, the ceremonies began on the Campus Martius under a full moon and by the light of torches. There were processions and prayers. Augustus sacrificed ewe lambs and kids to the Fates, a solemn and sacred rite, which ended in a banquet to Juno and Diana. The following day, June 1, was also passed in religious offices. At the Capitol, Augustus and Agrippa (who had married Augustus' daughter Julia and was recognized as his successor) each sacrificed a bullock to Jupiter Optimus Maximus. On the Campus Martius games and plays went on, and the day ended with a second banquet. At midnight cakes were offered to Ilithyia, goddess of childbirth.

On June 2, on the Capitoline Hill, Augustus and Agrippa each sacrificed a cow to Juno; and at night on the Campus Martius, Augustus offered up a pregnant sow to Mother Earth and implored her blessing. The next day, June 3, the ceremonies were performed on the Palatine Hill. In the temple to Apollo, Augustus and Agrippa made an offering of cakes to Apollo and Diana, and then as the culmination of the festival, came the hymn to the two deities, the *Carmen Saeculare*.

The hymn is written in the Sapphic meter and consists of nineteen stanzas, four lines each, to be sung by a choir of boys and a choir of girls, twenty-seven in each choir. It begins:

> Phoebe silvarumque potens Diana,
> lucidum caeli decus, o colendi
> semper et culti, date quae praecamur
>   tempore sacro,

> O Phoebus! and Diana goddess of woods!
> Radiant glories of the sky, O ever worshipful
> And always to be worshipped, grant the prayers
>   We pray at this holy season.

The stanzas address prayers severally to Apollo, to Ilithyia, to Ceres, to the Fates, and so on, sometimes the boys sing alone, sometimes the girls, and then again all together:

> Di, probos mores docili juventae,
> di, senectuti placidae quietem,
> Romulae genti date remque prolemque
>   et decus omne.

> O ye Gods, grant our youths virtuous ways,
> Make them accept them, grant to the old

Placid age, and to the people of Romulus
   Wealth and children and every honor.

May the glorious offspring of Anchises and Venus
   obtain what they pray for!
May the Parthians fear them!
May Indians and Scythians obey them!

Faith, Peace, Honor and a Humble Heart, and
Neglected Virtue have dared to come back,
And blessed Plenty appears with her full horn.
May Apollo, the Prophet, the Healer, prolong the
Prosperity of Rome and the happiness of Latium forever.

May Diana incline her heart to hear our prayers.

We, the music makers, the singers of hymns in
Honor of Phoebus and Diana, hold the sure hope
That Jove and all the Gods will hear our prayers.

Certain Latin scholars, taught to believe that a poem written
for a ceremonial function cannot be very good, do not speak
highly of the *Carmen Saeculare*. Composed upon command, it
must lack, they think, the force of personal or national emotion;
and they imply, if they do not say, that the poet as he writes his
verses will have some of his thoughts on the Emperor, some on
the singing choir or the chorus master, some on the priests, or
the parents of the children, others on the hot, weary, perspiring,
pushing, shoving crowd. But they forget that the poem was
written to be sung once, not to be read and studied in private.
If I dared to express an opinion, it would be that the hymn was
admirably adapted to the occasion, to be sung in the portico of
a temple, freshly resplendent with marble, the sweet young
voices of boys and girls echoing on into the cella and along the
coffered ceiling. It was for such a ceremony that the Latin
language was best adapted, and Horace composed his stanzas as
if he were architect of a spiritual temple.

A couple of years later Horace was called upon to compose two odes in honor of victories won by Tiberius and Drusus, sons of Livia and her first husband, Tiberius Claudius Nero. These two young men, especially Tiberius, were found to possess remarkable military capacity. There were wild and hostile tribes on the northern borders of Italy. Drusus marched northward over the Brenner Pass, while Tiberius came eastward from Gaul, crossed Lake Constance, effected a junction with his brother and in a brilliant and rapid campaign, subjugated what is now the Grisons and the Tyrol. These two odes and two more, which celebrated in extremely laudatory terms the glories of Augustus, were afterwards included in Book IV of the Odes. These eulogies on the Emperor, by a poet not given to exaggeration, schooled *luxuriantia compescere*, and written at a time when he wished nothing from the government, corroborate the statements I have already made concerning what Augustus meant to the Roman people.

XXII

ODES, BOOK IV

SUETONIUS says that Augustus urged Horace to add a fourth book of odes to his earlier three. This is no doubt true. And though the poet was lazy, due in part to advancing years, in part to imperfect health, he did so. The volume was published about 13 B.C.

The two most important odes in it were composed in honor of Tiberius and Drusus who had defeated wild peoples on the northern borders of Italy, as I have said. And the volume closes with a eulogy of Augustus himself. Horace's admiration of the great Emperor is charming in its ingenuous simplicity. It is pleasant to think of this little gentleman, short, stout, grizzled, sitting on the doorstep of his Sabine farm under the shade of the pine tree consecrated to Diana, his face lighting up as happy lines came to him, writing his last ode (Ode xv), joyful to think that he was contributing to a just estimate of the great Emperor:

I had wished to sing of battles, of cities conquered, but Apollo struck his lyre in loud rebuke, bade me not spread my little sails on a wide blustering sea.

Thou, Caesar, hast brought back ripe harvests to our fields. Thou hast torn from the proud temples of the Parthians, and restored to us, our standards. Thou hast shut the Temple of Janus. Thou hast bridled License that would overleap its lawful bounds. Thou hast cast out evil doing. Thou hast called back our ancient ways which caused the Latin name and the renowned might of Italy to grow great, and our majestic Empire to stretch from the rising of the sun to its bed in the west.

While Caesar guards the State, no civil fury, no violence, no wrath that on the smithy forges swords, and makes wretched cities enemies, shall do away with Peace. The Getae, the Seres, the Parthians, they that drink of the Danube, they that dwell by the River Don, shall obey the commands of Caesar. And we, upon our solemn holidays, yea, even on our working days, we, our children and our wives, with merry Bacchus pouring out his gifts, and ceremonial fit, shall invoke the Gods. Then, after our Fathers' fashion we will sing, mingling our voices with the Lydian flutes, of our dead heroes, of Troy, of Anchises and the descendants of dear Venus.

In this same book are two odes to Spring, Nos. VII and XII; the first is as charming as anything the poet wrote. There is also a poem (Odes IV, XI) on Maecenas' birthday which I have already quoted in part and will now give again.

> Phyllis dear, there is a jar of Alban wine
> that for more than nine years I have had.
> In the garden grows parsley meet to weave into garlands
> and a lush mass of ivy, which
> bound in your hair will make you radiantly lovely.
> The house is gay with glistening silver; the altar,
> decked with immaculate leaves, is ready
> for the sacrificial lamb.
>
> The whole household bustles about, the maids
> and men-servants in confusion rush hither
> and thither, the flames flicker and flash
> as they roll the sooty smoke up in a
> whirling column.

And now you must know to what great festival
you are bid. You are to celebrate the Ides
of April, the midday of seaborn Venus's
              favorite month,

a sacred day for me, as is most meet, more
to be kept with proper ritual almost than
my own natal day, for from this day
              my dear Maecenas reckons his passing years.

Come, last of my Loves — for I shall never love
another woman — learn my songs and sing them
with your dear, dear voice.
              Songs drive Black Care away.

There is one aspect of this book that has drawn to itself, more
than the other aspects, the attention of the commentators. They
point to the fact that there is but one ode to Maecenas, and contrast this paucity with the poet's trumpet-like salutation at the
beginning of the first epistle in Book I:

Prima dicte mihi, summa dicende Camena . . . Maecenas.

Maecenas! whom my Muse praised at the first, and at
the last shall praise.

They infer from this that there was a coolness, perhaps an
estrangement, between these two. They seek justification in a
statement by Dio Cassius that in 16 B.C. Maecenas fell out of
favor with Augustus and retired into private life, and, at least
as I understand it, they advance to the conclusion that Horace
sided with the Emperor and shared his estrangement from
Maecenas. These arguments do not persuade me at all. There
are on the record but two matters that might have caused a rift
between Augustus and Maecenas, both connected wtih the latter's wife Terentia. The first is that Terentia's brother Murena
was discovered to be concerned in a plot with Fannius Caepio on

the Emperor's life. Maecenas was informed of Murena's complicity, and told Terentia. Tiberius brought the prosecution, both men were convicted and executed. Maecenas, of course, ought not to have told Terentia, though it is conceivable that he entertained a hope that she might be able to do or say something that would save Murena's life, or persuade him to confess all the details of his plot. At all events that affair had taken place in the year 23 B.C. and was, by the time the fourth book was published in 13 B.C., ancient history.

The other reason is that gossip talked scandal about Augustus and Terentia. Dio Cassius some two hundred years later, was, so far as I can make out, the first author who has come down to us to circulate the story. He says Terentia travelled with Augustus in Gaul. Buchan thinks the story improbable. I denounce it as nonsense. If it were true Suetonius would certainly have paraded it. Augustus was fond of Maecenas — long after Maecenas' death when he was in trouble, he exclaimed, "Had Maecenas been alive this would not have happened." He loved his wife Livia — Suetonius says *Liviam . . . dilexit et probavit unice ac perserveranter*, "he loved and esteemed Livia always and only her" — and he had issued strong edicts against adultery, the *Lex Julia de adulteriis coercendis* had recently been enacted. In Ode v of this very book Horace praises him because

> nullis polluitur casta domus stupris,
>
> The home is pure, unstained by bestialities;

and, as I have already remarked, the Emperor announced his intention of leaving a worthy example for the next generation.

One must remember that there are a great many persons, historical writers among them, who prefer scandal to truth.

I believe that Dio confounded cause and effect. Maecenas withdrew from public life of his own free will, and Dio jumped to the conclusion that he had lost favor with the Emperor.

Suetonius says, "For more than forty years Augustus used the
same bedroom in winter and summer . . . but whenever he
was not well, he slept at Maecenas' house," without any suggestion of any intermission. The simplest theory is that Maecenas
had worked very hard, he was over fifty years old, he had accomplished his work, the monarchy was established, and he
wished for ease. He was not robust. The elder Pliny says he
had frequent fevers and for the last three years of his life never
slept at all. Besides, Maecenas disliked to live in the blaze of
public life, he was a gentleman and liked privacy. Propertius
says, in an epistle (Elegies, II, 1) to him:

You bid me attempt some conspicuous work, but you yourself shrink from
all publicity. As a magistrate in Rome you might parade lictors and dis-
pense justice in the Forum; you might decorate your walls with captured
spears; and yet, though Caesar gives you full powers, though riches lie at
your disposal, you hang back and humbly hide yourself in the shadowy
background. Believe me, your modesty will rival that of Camillus.

This love of privacy was one of the traits that brought
Maecenas and Horace together. The reader will remember how
Horace says to Maecenas, "I shuddered, and with good reason,
at the thought of publicity," *late conspicuum tollere verticem*
(Odes III, xvi). Horace retired to the Sabine farm, but
Maecenas out of loyalty to Augustus, did not feel at liberty to
withdraw into private life until the Empire was well organized.
This view is confirmed by the conversation which Tacitus records
as having taken place between Seneca and Nero, at the time
when Seneca wished to withdraw from the imperial service.
Seneca says: "Your illustrious ancestor, Augustus, permitted
Marcus Agrippa to retire to Mytilene; he allowed Maecenas to
live almost a stranger in Rome, and dwell in the heart of the
city as it were in solitude." Nero replied: "It is true, Augustus
released Agrippa and Maecenas from the fatigue of business,

etc." It is clear that Tacitus thought that Maecenas withdrew voluntarily and was not dismissed. (I have quoted Arthur Murray's translation of Tacitus' Annals, book XIV, chapter xxxxv.)

I find no evidence of any estrangement, other than that which of necessity arises from the fact that men who take different paths, one a private lane and the other the world's highroad, cannot walk together. When Maecenas died he left all his property to Augustus (8 B.C.).

And even if there was a coolness between Maecenas and Augustus, it does not follow that there was also a coolness between Maecenas and Horace. If Dio is right and Maecenas had fallen into disfavor, Horace would have been the last man to abandon his best friend for the sake of imperial grace. The only evidence of coolness lies in the absence of any odes to Maecenas in Book IV, other than the birthday ode. But it is obvious that had Horace inserted other odes to Maecenas he would have run counter to the purpose with which he composed the book. The Emperor had asked him to compose it. He asked him for the odes on Tiberius and Drusus, and Horace as virtual poet laureate also put in two odes in honor of the Emperor, and made the whole a sort of poet laureate performance.

Three bits of evidence testify on the positive side. One is the birthday ode, which was probably written, to judge from its place in the book, about 15 B.C. The second is a statement by Suetonius: "How fond Maecenas was of Horace is evident enough from the epigram — If I do not love you, Horace, more than my life, look at your old friend as leaner than Ninnius (obviously a scare-crow of a man)." And third, when he came to die, Maecenas bade Augustus to be as mindful of Horace, as of himself, which is really conclusive evidence that there was no coolness then between any of the three.

To me the book lacks, except for the ode *Diffugere nives,* the fresh grace that gilds the earlier books with so rich a patina.

XXIII

THE PHILOSOPHER

Lovers of Horace like him and admire him as a lyrical poet. They wonder at the skill with which he put those hard, unbending, almost truculent Latin words into such delicate sequences. His lovers learn three or four odes by heart, perhaps five or six, for every lover of Horace is a picker and chooser, but, as a rule, they find only a few that completely satisfy their appetite for lyrical elegance. One man's favorite is *Fons Bandusiae*, another's the lament on the death of Quintilius, another's is that on Regulus — but though his readers differ about his lyrics, all are agreed in commending and enjoying his philosophy.

Philosophy is rather an academic word for the heterogeneous compilation of bits of common sense that Horace gathered together, drew upon, and gave out here and there in his kindly meditative fashion. I never take up his first book of Epistles without regretting that tobacco had not been discovered in his time. If ever a man should have had a pipe, it was Horace. A pipe is almost necessary to make secure the basis of a philosophy like his. His thoughts were such as are bred in part from conversation with a few friends, but in the main from puffing on a solitary pipe, letting ideas flutter down as the smoke rises in successive cloudlets, lingers, mounts in the air, and dissolves.

His basic theories were fetched from Epicurus' garden. He cared not at all for physics. Atoms might do what they liked as far as he was concerned, he ignored logic. As for religion, he says that Lucretius taught him that the gods lead a carefree life and he left it at that. His philosophy was a philosophy of conduct. There is not much use in trying to find a linked sequence of ideas, a *hence*, a *therefore* and *it follows*. He flutters here and there zigzagging, as I have said, like a butterfly — a Matinian bee is his expression. Nevertheless, I shall follow and pick out happy phrases and clinquant words, and try to present them in some kind of orderly fashion.

I hesitate to put a note of sadness first, for sadness certainly does not predominate, but I think that after reading the Odes, one feels that Horace is always conscious that "our little life is rounded by a sleep." Death keeps whispering, "I am not far away." Horace is not afraid, he merely bids us not to forget this (Odes I, IV).

> Pallida Mors aequo pulsat pede pauperum tabernas
> regumque turres.

> Pale Death with impartial foot knocks at the
> Cottages of the poor and the palaces of the rich.

Again, in the poem to Postumus (Odes II, XIV) he says,

> Eheu fugaces, Postume, Postume,
> labuntur anni, nec pietas moram
> rugis et instanti senectae
> adferet indomitaeque morti.

> Alas, Postumus, Postumus,
> The years slip by,
> And duty done will not delay wrinkles, or
> The onslaught of old age, or Death the conqueror.

Of course these black thoughts come at intervals, and they are not black to him. As day and night constitute one whole, so do life and death. Death is as natural as life, and, in spite of fanciful tales of Sisyphus, Ixion, the daughters of Danaus, is by no means to be feared. I quote from Odes I, xxviii:

> Omnis una manet nox,
> et calcanda semel via leti.

> One universal night awaits us all,
> The path of death must once be trodden.

This thought of death, as I say, is solemn but not sad, and always, or nearly always, brings with it the connotation of man's common humanity, of human brotherhood, because we all share in the noble experience of death; since death is impartial, since it at the end renders us all free and equal, why should there not be more freedom and equality during this fitful fever which is life?

But there is another connotation, more conspicuous than that I have just mentioned. If death is the end, and comes no man knows when, then while we live let us enjoy life. *Carpe diem*, make the most of today, *quam minimum credula postero* (Odes I, xi), "trust tomorrow as little as possible"; *quid sit futurum cras, fuge quaerere* (Odes I, ix), "keep from asking what will happen in the future." This is the very essence of Epicureanism. The Christian, the Mohammedan, bids us trust in the unknown, the unknowable, future; the Stoic bids us be strenuous for the noble; but the Epicurean says, with a gentle ironical smile, "Let us put our trust in what we hear, and see, and feel, and gather roses while we may." As Horace says (Odes III, viii):

> Dona praesentis cape laetus horae ac linque severa
>
> Be glad to take what gifts the passing
> Hour bestows, and leave sad things alone.

The next article of his creed follows in logical sequence as a corollary of the second. To make the most of life, *carpere diem*, one must follow the golden mean, *aurea mediocritas*, the doctrine of Aristotle. *Virtus est medium vitiorum et utrimque reductum* (Epis. I, xviii), "virtue is midway between opposite vices." One must live one's life on an even keel. Steer the middle way, the poet says (Odes II, x):

> Rectius vives, Licini, neque altum
> semper urgendo neque, dum procellas
> cautus horrescis, nimium premendo
> litus iniquum.
>
> You will live more wisely, Licinius,
> If you do not always head for open sea
> Or hug the dangerous shore in
> Cautious fear of storms.

He reiterates the point (Odes II, iii):

> Aequam memento rebus in arduis
> servare mentem, non secus in bonis
> ab insolenti temperatam
> laetitia, moriture Delli.
>
> Remember, Dellius, for death will come,
> When things go hard, keep your heart steady,
> And in prosperity, untouched
> By violent joy.

Est modus in rebus (Sat. I, i), "there is a measure in everything" — a simple saying, but simplicity is no bad quality, and it is no simpler than remarks by Montaigne, Ben Franklin, or Will Rogers.

Such then, is the substance of Horace's philosophy: enjoy life while we can, but so act in enjoying today's happiness as not to hinder tomorrow's. And to this he adds, casually, here and there various little apothegms from his experience. I will cite a number of examples, culled from different works.

> Non semper idem floribus est honor
> vernis (Odes II, xi).

> In flowers the glory of the spring
> Does not stay fixed.

>   Patriae quis exsul
> se quoque fugit? (Odes II, xvi).

> You can escape from your country,
> But can you escape from yourself?

> Destrictus ensis cui super impia
> cervice pendet, non Siculae dapes
>   dulcem elaborabunt saporem,
>   non avium citheraeque cantus
> somnum reducent (Odes III, i).

> For him, over whose impious head
> A drawn sword hangs, no feasts Sicilian
> Can compound a savor sweet,
>   No lute, nor song of birds,
> Bring back his sleep.

> Quid leges sine moribus
>   vanae proficiunt (Odes III, xxiv).

> What can vain laws without morals accomplish?

Minuentur atrae
carmine curae (Odes IV, xi).

Poetry diminishes black care.

Mihi res, non me rebus, subjungere conor (Epis. I, i).

I try to subject circumstances to me,
Not myself to circumstances.

Et genus et forman regina Pecunia donat (Epis. I, vi).

Money, our queen, bestows both birth and beauty.

Imperat aut servit collecta pecunia cuique (Epis. I, x).

Your money, piled up, is your master or your servant.

Sedit qui timuit ne non succederet (Epis. I, xvii).

He sits still, who fears to fall.

That is enough. You see how admirably the compact Latin
words serve the poet's purpose, how economical the means, how
luxuriant the effect. And his art is equally brilliant in what I
call his clinquant words: *simplex munditiis, splendide mendax,
purpureus pannus.* How could two words call up livelier images? *Simplex munditiis* (Odes I, v), you can see Pyrrha before
her glass, tying up her golden hair, knowing well that absence
of ornaments enhances her native beauty. *Splendide mendax*
(Odes III, xi), words that show how falsehood can shine
brighter than truth. And how would caviling critics be able to
deride, or delighted readers be able to praise, some Paolo Vero-
nese burst of rhetoric, had they not had the phrase, "The Purple
Patch," *pannus purpureus?*

XXIV

HORACE'S ART

THE man who has a liking for poetry, who knows he is not one of the *cognoscenti*, and also that he does not wish to be guided by *cognoscenti*, and is therefore forced back upon his own resources, usually draws a line between two categories of poets. My two categories are these. There are poets who like to stay at home, and there are poets that like to leave home seeking adventure. By home, I mean not merely the home where the man was born, nor the place of one's earliest memories, the garden of heliotrope and Shirley poppies, the trees which he climbed, nor the horizon line, or friendships and first love, or earliest acquaintance with Shakespeare, Scott, Dickens, nor high resolves made, neglected, broken, and regretted, nor one's school, schoolmates, college, country, but rather the sum of all familiar things, all that has surrounded and encompassed his body, heart, and mind.

Poets of the second sort fly from the nest, they seek new things, they go in quest of adventures — moral, intellectual, spiritual — they pursue what they are fond of calling "reality" or "truth," they feed on hope, they live in tomorrow, they prefer the possible to the commonplace, and the impossible to the possible, they carry a thyrsus and wrap their senses in the mystical, they despise what is so dear to the first group, the *déjà connu*. The two groups are like children, one prefers to play with its nursery hobby-horse, the other to swing higher and higher.

To make my division clearer, I will cite a supreme instance of the second category: Dante. Such a one disdains the familiar, the common; he finds joy in the great adventures of Right and Wrong, and their glorious strife; he will not tarry, he presses on, forward, forward; he knows no bounds between matter and mind, between the evidence of the senses and the imaginings of the spirit; he feeds on honeydew and drinks the milk of Paradise. The tangible, the seeable, the hearable have no limitations for him. Dante deceived himself into thinking he wanted peace, order, ease, a home — he wanted war, war, against Devils and Laodiceans, he sighed for Florence, but he set his heart on *quella Roma onde Christo è Romano*.

Of the first group — the poets who stay at home — Homer, he of the Odyssey if there be two Homers, is the great exemplar. Ulysses represents the author's attitude toward life, he has his eyes and thoughts on what he has earliest known and loved: on the surroundings of his boyhood, the rocky Island of Ithaca, its goats, its goatherds, on Penelope, Telemachus, on Argos, his hound, and all that he associated with home. No matter what his adventures, his mishaps, his griefs, no matter how beautiful in their native dress the goddesses that woo him, his thoughts are always fixed on home, and he sits on the salt sea sands, turns his eyes towards Ithaca, and is sick at heart.

Horace possesses these classical qualities that belonged to Homer — breadth, dignity, serenity — but I do not mean to make a claim of any close relation between the two. Horace, true Roman that he was, was absolutely pure of mysticism, he would have looked very blank had you handed him Isaiah, whereas Virgil would have been interested though not sympathetic. Horace was not religious, using that word in a transcendental sense. The phrase "Nearer, my God, to Thee," would have puzzled him greatly. Nor did he care for humanity, as zealots do who are unable to give their hearts to God, hoping like Abou Ben Adhem, that it means much the same thing. Rome, *Roma Immortalis*, was the farthest bourne of his most exalted moments. Heroism he praised, but had you asked him as he sat under Diana's pine tree beside his farm home, he would have given you an ironical answer. Passion he did not know, winged emotions he had no experience of, he watched them as he would watch clouds riding through the sky, with cool appreciation, he preferred the solid earth. I was about to add William Blake as the antipode from Horace, when I chanced to come upon a phrase of Blake's, that I should like to borrow for Horace, "The great and golden rule of art, as well as of life, is this: That the more distinct, sharp, and wirey the bounding line, the more perfect the work of art." Horace always keeps his bounding line distinct and sharp.

It is idle to write what a man is not, but it is hard to fence him about otherwise — you describe what is within him, by enumerating what is without. Such a description of Horace will fill a proud index: A kind heart, and no sentimentality; a just mind, readier to err on the side of generosity than of severity; a pious enjoyment of the good things of life — *ars fruendi* — for he made his blithe pilgrimage through this world grateful for youth and health, for the power to run and leap, for beautiful Greek verses written long since by poets across the sea, for peace and order, for a farm, for an honest bailiff, for the juice of grapes stored in casks and jugs, and poured out rutilant under bright sunshine in all the glory of color, for pretty girls, coy and not coy, for dear friends, for his own talents, for fields and woods *tacitum silvas inter reptare salubres*. If you will give the word religious its fullest significance, Horace was religious in his conscious enjoyment of all these things.

> The world is so full of a number of things
> I'm sure we should all be as happy as kings,

and Horace was. And he had a Puritanical conscience for his art, picking out words to match his thoughts, examining their syllables, sometimes mindful of their texture and occasionally of such music as l's and r's and m's and n's and short and long vowels can give, "not speaking words as they chanceably fall from the mouth but pryzing each syllable of each word by just proportion according to the dignitie of the subject."

He never mounted Pegasus but rode the good cob common sense, saddled and bridled by human experience. He set no value on a sick man's dreams, *aegri somnia*, and his pronouncement,

> Scribendi recte sapere est et principium et fons,

though applied to the drama, he would, no doubt, extend to all poetry.

Sapere I take to be human knowledge, based on our senses, and not on the traveller tales of mystics journeying beyond time and space, and good poetry, perhaps the best, springs from it. Horace never attempts matters beyond his reach. *Sumite materiam vestris, qui scribitis, aequam viribus.* Mackail speaks of his "subtle psychological insight." I am at a loss to understand this expression, unless he means that Horace puts words in happy juxtaposition, as a painter would different colors, so that each, both by its meaning, and sometimes by its sound, should affect its neighbor and produce a subtle, often a poetical effect. But the characters of men or women he brings in, whether real or imaginary, are depicted broadly and simply. He did not write

an epic or tragedies — no *Epipsychidion*, no *Hound of Heaven*
— but odes and epistles. He never was encumbered by that
unfortunate phrase of Matthew Arnold, "To see life whole,"
knowing as he did, that there is your life, and my life, and
Tom's life, and Dick's life, but that the platonic abstraction *life*,
however useful in logic, varies like clouds according to the mind
that contemplates it, changing with every season, with every
vivid experience. *Quot homines tot sententiae.* Horace dwelt
among the concrete, and never essayed to fly, *pinnis non homini
datis.* Poets he says wish either to please or do good, to say
things both pleasant and helpful to life. (A.P., lines 333–334.)

But, I repeat, it is idle to harp on what a man is not. And it
would require a far more penetrating intelligence than I possess
to make a complete inventory of Horace's capacities. Chief
among them is his deft and elegant arrangement of words, for
he uses them as if they were precious stones. "If Oratio next to
Ratio, Speech next to Reason, bee the greatest gyft bestowed
upon mortalitie, that cannot be praiseless which doth most pol-
lish that blessing of speech which considers each word, not only
(as a man may say) by his [its] forcible quality but by his [its]
best measured quantitie, carrying even in themselves a Har-
monie."

Sir Philip Sidney is right, Horace's conciseness charms us
with that husbandry of effort, which for some reason is dear to
our subconscious conscience. And incidentally, he says that a *vir
bonus et prudens* will scold lifeless verses, will blame them if
harsh, will strike out those devoid of grace, make the obscure
clear, cut out pretentious ornament, condemn ambiguity (A.P.,
lines 445–450). I fear he would have regarded Blake as a
poeta vesanus.

Horace is no poet of the soul, no practiser of "beautiful, wild,
feline" poetry, he is the poet of civilized man — of the commonplace man, if you like — not of Crashaw, St. John of the

Apocalypse, Emily Dickinson, not of men centrifugal, seeking to escape the laws of human gravity. He does not dance, he walks; he does not sing, but talks, talks with the persuasive cadences of Apollo and Diana when they are in high discourse. He is the poet, not of love but of friendship, he does not address Romeo, Ferdinand, Florizel, but the unspiritual, the unromantic, the ordinary, and yet not altogether ordinary, wingless man, to win him to untroubled thoughts. This aristocratic love of elegance, his serious acceptance of art as a great responsibility, as a matter of measure, proportion, of the golden mean, his belief in reason and good sense, are what today more than ever the aspirants to art, the aspirants to civilization, need.

For many people, especially the old and middle-aged, it is pleasant to leave the great adventurous steppes of poetry, rimmed though they be with jagged mountains, and enriched here and there with a feather dropped by an eagle, and enter a sunny brick-walled garden, to find a fig tree espaliered, a fragrance of mignonette, a bed of wind-swept, jaunty Shirley poppies, ease and peace. But that is a matter of temperament and taste. *Non est disputandium.*

XXV

HIS FAME

LIKE other philosophers Horace has various moods, or perhaps I should say, various aspects to his character; at one time he verges upon cynicism, at another upon stoicism. And, *per contra*, after reading the first book of Epistles, one says the key to his character is clubability. And there is much to say in support of that theory. His long list of friends: Maecenas *et praesidium et dulce decus meum*, Pollio *cui laurus aeternus honores Delmatico peperit triumpho*, Virgil *animae dimidium meae*, Sestius, *o beate Sesti*, Varius *Maeonii carminis ales*, *dulcis* Lamia, Plancus, Varus, etc., offer convincing proof. He was the life of a dinner party, the gayest at a picnic on the banks of the Digentia. How delightful to see him unsealing a cask, and listen to him hum the tune as Lyde played the lute and sang one of his *carmina!*

There was another aspect, of course, as often happens with those blessed with the gift of gaiety, he had his liking for solitude. No one who knows him could imagine that he should covet a villa at Tibur. He had many a moment when he wished to be alone, to stroll in his woods or upland meadows, or sit silent beside the Digentia and watch its waters swirl and sway as they flowed by.

It is this double-sidedness that has made him so popular from his own lifetime until today, or had I better say till the end of the nineteenth century, for the twentieth century with its child-like admiration for the achievements of applied science has, it seems, pushed the classics to the wall.

Horace's fame has had a romance of its own, following the fortunes of the Roman Empire; about this, however, we have but scraps of information. Petronius, clever man, speaks of his *curiosa felicitas*, and Quintilian, the great Latin critic, says: "Of our lyric poets Horace is about the only one worth reading; for he sometimes reaches real heights, and he is at the same time full of delightfulness and grace, and both in variety of imagery and in words is most happily daring" (Showerman's translation). Suetonius' *Life* is a poor thing, containing scarcely any information not found in Horace's poems, except extracts from imperial letters. Pomponius Porphyrio — what a delightful name for a scholiast! — gives some information concerning persons and things mentioned in the poems, but when the Dark Ages drew the "gradual dusky veil" of indifference over things of the mind, Horace was nearly forgotten. Here and there in monasteries manuscripts were copied and his memory preserved. With the dawn of the revival of learning he was again quoted. I am told that in the twelfth century the Epistles and Satires were quoted five hundred and twenty times and the Odes seventy-seven. And for the thirteenth century (I quote a chance memory) when the great Hohenstaufen Emperor of the Holy Roman Empire, Frederick II, *Stupor Mundi*, was at deadly strife with the Papacy, he wrote to his fellow sovereigns in Christendom, seeking their help, and quoted: "*Nam tua res agitur, paries cum proximus ardet* (Epis. I, xviii), your property is in danger when your neighbor's house is on fire."

Dante places him, *Orazio Satiro,* next to Homer in the little band of poets in Limbo. Petrarch hailed him:

> Salve, o dei lirici modi sovrano,
> Salve, o degl' Itali gloria ed onor!

> Hail, Sovereign of lyric measures,
> Hail, glory and honor of the Italians!

Shakespeare quoted him (*Titus Andronicus,* Act IV, Scene 2). And since then he has been quoted in every land by illustrious writers. In France, Montaigne, Fénelon, Boileau, and La Fontaine head the list, and Voltaire said he was the best of preachers. In England the eighteenth century — Addison, Pope, Dr. Johnson, Lord Chesterfield, and many more — made much of him.

But the admiration that Horace himself would have liked best is that shown him by those poets who, to quote his own words, *apis Matinae more modoque,* sucked drops of honey from his poems for their own use. I will mention some that I have noticed.

Petrarch borrowed from Odes I, xxii:

> Dulce ridentem Lalagen amabo,
> dulce loquentem

to write of Laura,

> Non sa com' Amor sana e com' ancide,
> Chi non sa come dolce ella sospira,
> E come dolce parla, e come dolce ride.

And when Michael Angelo in his sonnet on Dante said:

> Simil o maggior uom' non nacque mai,

there must have been lingering in the back of his mind the lines from Odes I, xii:

> Unde nil majus generatur ipso,
> nec viget quicquam simile aut secundum.

I have shown how Ronsard for his poem, *La Fontaine Bellerie*, borrowed from *Fons Bandusiae*. And Milton must have remembered from Odes III, IV, great Latin scholar that he was,

> Qui rore puro Castaliae lavit
> crines solutos

when he says of the resuscitated Lycidas

> With nectar pure his oozy locks he laves.

Alexander Pope imitated Horace from earliest years, his:

> Get place and wealth; if possible with grace,
> If not, by any means get wealth and place,

translates from Epistles I, 1:

> Rem facias, rem,
> si possis, recte, si non, quocumque modo, rem,

even more directly than our modern American version, "Get on, my boy, honestly if you can, but get on."

The thought,

> Nihil est ab omni parte beatum
> Nothing is perfect in every part,

must have been in the back of Goethe's mind, when the poignant utterance bursts from poor Faust, *O dass dem Menschen nicht volkomnes wird, empfind ich nun.*

Of such borrowings a great number could be readily discovered.

Horace, himself, felt confident of his future fame. *Exegi monumentum aere perennius* (Odes III, xxx). He foretold (Odes II, xx) that his name would be known on the shores of the Bosphorus, in North Africa, among the Hyperboreans, on the borders of the Black Sea, in Thrace, in Dacia, in Spain, and along the banks of the Rhine. But he did not anticipate that, when the Pontifex Maximus attended by the silent Vestal had long ceased to climb the Capitoline Hill, his name would still be a household word not merely in the regions that he knew but in vast countries he had never dreamed of.

There is little to say of his later years. The great figures of his lifetime were passing away. Agrippa died in 12 B.C., Octavia the next year, Drusus two years later, and Maecenas at the end of September, 8 B.C. Long years before, perhaps twenty, Horace had written to Maecenas (Odes II, xvii) that if fate should first take his friend (*meae pars animae*, part of my soul), he, the other part, would not linger on. "That day shall bring the doom of both." And so it nearly turned out, for within two months after Maecenas' death, on November 27th, Horace died of some sudden illness, lacking ten days of fifty-seven years. He left no written will, but by word of mouth named Augustus as his heir. His body was buried on the farther end of the Esquiline Hill near the tomb of Maecenas, but his spirit is lodged in the great Pantheon of civilization.

Aux grands hommes, l'humanité reconnaissante.

His memory remains green, not because he was a gifted poet of long ago in a dead language, nor because he was one of the famous men of the most dominant nation in history at the time of its brightest glory, but because in trouble and in prosperity, in hours of mirth or in boredom, his art, his philosophy and his loving kindliness bring men to serenity, at peace with the world and themselves.

Ave, lauriger Horati, et vale!

For he's a jolly good fellow,
For he's a jolly good fellow,
For he's a jolly good fellow,
As nobody can deny.

It is in their literature that the inner spirit of the Latin race found its most complete expression. In the stately structure of that imperial language they embodied those qualities which make the Roman name most abidingly great — honour, temperate wisdom, humanity, courtesy, magnanimity; and the civilized world still returns to that fountainhead.

J. W. Mackail

APPENDICES

A

A VILLA AT TIBUR?

SOME scholars hold that in addition to the Sabine farm Horace owned a villa at Tibur (Tivoli). The theory is based on a statement of Suetonius, the author of a short "Life of Horace," written about one hundred and forty years after the alleged acquisition of the estate at Tibur. It does not appear that Suetonius made any special investigations, and the information which he gives was probably derived from the poems themselves or from mere hearsay. There is nothing to imply that he had ever been to the Sabine Valley, and one must remember that he reports miraculous omens with the same assurance that he describes the situation of Horace's house.

Suetonius says: *Vixit plurimum in secessu ruris sui Sabini aut Tiburtini, domusque eius ostenditur circa Tiburni luculum,* "Horace lived most of the time in the retirement of his Sabine or Tiburtine country place; and his house is pointed out near Tiburnus' copse."

I had better confess here, in order to show my prejudice, that I half suspect that in this passage Suetonius confounded Horace with Catullus. In one of his odes Catullus addresses his farm:

> O funde noster, seu Sabine seu Tiburs,
> (nam te esse Tiburtem autumant, quibus non est
> cordi Catullum laedere: at quibus cordi est
> quovis Sabinum pignore esse contendunt)
> sed seu Sabine sive verius Tiburs,
> fui libenter in tua suburbana
> villa

Dear Farm (They that do not wish to vex Catullus say you are Tiburtine, they that do will wager any stakes that you are Sabine), but whether you are Sabine or more properly Tiburtine, I was glad to be in your house near the city.

These verses were of just the kind to stick in Suetonius' memory, a man wholly devoid of any notion of poetry; and being told that the house was pointed out, *domus eius ostenditur,* he clutched at the confused memory, and, conscious that he knew almost nothing of Horace's life, wrote his rash statement, indifferent to any possible consequence of misleading English scholars.

I repeat, Suetonius' statement is all the evidence we have except for inferences drawn from Horace's poems. Let us see what he does say about Tibur. In his ode to his friend Plancus (Odes I, vii), Horace praises Tibur: "As for me, not hardy Lacedaemon, nor the rich fields of Larisa have impressed me so forcibly as the echoing house of Albunea, and the headlong Anio, and the grove of Tiburnus and the orchards watered by the running rills." These places are indeed at Tibur, but Horace does not speak as a proprietor of land there; quite the contrary, he calls Tibur *Tibur tuum,* Plancus' Tibur, not his.

The sixth ode in Book II, addressed to Septimius, is also in praise of Tibur, but of Tarentum much more. Horace exclaims:

> Tibur . . .
> sit meae sedes utinam senectae

Would that Tibur were to be the seat of my old age! But if that cannot be, I will go to that corner of the world beside the river Galaesus in Lucania, which more than all others smiles on me, where the honey equals that of Hymettus, the olives vie with those of Venafrum, where springs are long and winters mild and the grapes envy not those of Falernum. That place calls to thee and me. There shalt thou drop a tear on my ashes.

The supporters of the hypothesis that Horace owned a villa at Tibur attach much weight to the phrase,

> Tibur . . .
> sit meae sedes utinam senectae

But let them turn to the lines in the eleventh epistle of Book I:

> Scis Lebedus quid sit: Gabiis disertior atque
> Fidenis vicus; tamen illic vivere vellem.
> oblitusque meorum, obliviscendus et illis,
> Neptunuum procul e terra spectare furentem.

You know what Lebedus is: a town more desolate than Gabii or Fidenae; yet there I should love to live, and, forgetting my friends, and forgotten by them, gaze from the land far out at the raging sea.

Here is the expression of a wish to live at Lebedus as fervent as the wish to live at Tibur. Why take either *au pied de la lettre*?

Horace expressed a wish to pass his old age at Tibur, and these aforesaid theorists infer that Maecenas took the hint. But is it clear that by "Tibur" Horace means the town? Is he not thinking of the whole valley? He is not classifying two towns together, Tibur and Tarentum, as admirable places, but two districts, the Tiburtine and the Tarentine. To be sure he speaks carelessly, or under the obligation of versification, so that at first reading it seems as if he refers to Tibur as a town, but it is with the Tarentine countryside that he compares it, as is obvious from the description, and thereby shows that when he said "Tibur"

he meant the district. I am informed that every Italian municipality was a county as well as a city; one name would serve for
both.

From the town of Tibur to the Sabine farm is but eight miles
as the crow flies, not a great distance to include under one ap-
pellation. Horace does the same elsewhere. He speaks of fertile
Tibur, and fertile is an adjective that pertains to a country district, not a town. And in Epistles I, xvi, when describing the
Sabine farm, he says: *Dicas adductum propius frondere Tarentum*, "you would say that Tarentum had been brought near and
was in full foliage." Here Tarentum obviously does not mean
the municipality but the countryside about it.

Another ode to examine is the second in Book IV. In it
Horace says: "In my poor way I compose laborious poems after
the manner of a Matinian bee that works hard to gather sweet
thyme about the grove and banks of the well-watered Tibur."
The Tiburtine theory interprets this passage to mean that
Horace wrote his poems at Tibur. Wishful imaginings! What
he says is that he labors after the manner of the Matinian bee
(*apis Matinae more modoque*); the bee, however, did not hive
at Tibur but at Matinum in Apulia. The passage hardly justifies
any inference that the poet possessed a villa at Tibur.

The theorists also use the third ode in Book IV for their
argument. Here the poet says: If the Muse Melpomene smiles
on a man-child at birth, that child will not win fame as a boxer
or charioteer, or as a conquering soldier, but "the waters that
flow past fertile Tibur, and the thick foliage of its groves will
make him a notable poet." As before, I believe Horace used the
word "Tibur" to indicate the countryside and not the town. The
phrase "the waters that flow past fertile Tibur" is but a poetical
paraphrase for the River Anio, and the groves are the woodland round about. At all events the verses afford inadequate evidence of ownership of any villa.

In the Epistles there are but two references to Tibur. In Book I, VII, it appears that Maecenas has invited Horace to go to Rome. Horace excuses himself: He says, "Little things are suitable for little people. At present I don't hanker for imperial Rome, *sed vacuum Tibur placet aut imbelle Tarentum,* but I like leisurely Tibur or peaceful Tarentum." There is no suggestion of owning a villa. I infer that the epistle was written at his Sabine farm, and means: If you had invited me to Tibur or Tarentum I might have accepted, but to Rome, no thank you.

Now there is but one reference to Tibur left; that occurs in Epistle I, VIII, which was presumably written about 21 B.C. It is addressed to Celsus Albinovanus, and I have already quoted it at length in Chapter XIX. The words which are important to the argument are these: "At Rome I love Tibur, at Tibur I love Rome." But this sentence is but a variation of *Romae rus optas; absentem rusticus urbem tollis ad astra levis* (Sat. II, VII), "at Rome you long for the country; in the country you praise the city to the skies, you fickle fellow!" The reader must remember that Horace was obliged to use words that fitted with his meter.

In those years Horace wrote, not merely for close friends, but for a large public. The Sabine farm had no village or town address. People who had never visited it would have but a hazy idea of Mons Lucretilis or the River Digentia, whereas the name Tibur was known everywhere, and indicated not merely the town but the whole countryside.

One of the main points in my judgment that the assertion that Horace possessed a villa at Tibur is an error, and a grave error, is that it indirectly accuses Horace of inconsistency, or worse, of a certain hypocrisy. The poet was always preaching the simple life — moderation, plain living — and he rebuked luxury and riches. If, besides his home or apartment at Rome, where he had

at least three slaves, besides his Sabine farm, with five tenants
and eight slaves, he also possessed a villa at fashionable Tibur,
he would obviously be a member of a rich and luxurious class
whose customs he disapproved. I feel it a duty to Horace's
memory to deny possession of a villa at Tibur and to give my
reasons.

Horace would not have wanted a house at Tibur. Tibur was
for the rich and fashionable. The great lived there. Brutus and
Cassius lived there, and members of the Scipio family, as well
as the ill-fated Varus. Horace liked independence, simplicity,
books, freedom from uninvited society. If he stayed in Tibur
longer than a visit he would have felt as if he were in prison.
Can you for a moment imagine him a permanent guest in
Maecenas' luxurious house, ministered to by a multitude of unnecessary slaves, jostled by important visitors social and political?
Where would Horace go for privacy, for a tête-à-tête, or to read
a book, or meditate over a poem? And suppose the lady of the
house, Terentia, were there — handsome, vivacious, demanding
admiration, flirting, as gossip said she did, over freely? What
then? Would Horace submit to being treated as a lion; to have
her inviting strangers to dinner: "My dear Balbus, you really
must come and meet our brilliant and charming poet-philoso-
pher"? No, even if Horace had had the house to himself while
his host and hostess were away, his residence there for more than
a short visit would be unthinkable.

Let us see if any further light can be found in the poems. I
have already examined those that spoke of Tibur town itself,
but perhaps inferences may be drawn from some of the others.
The date of the grant is assumed to be 27 B.C., and it is possible
that one or two of the odes I cite may have been written before
that date and therefore carry no weight as evidence, but the prob-
ability seems to be that all were written later.

Odes II, xvi. Here the poet says that Fate has given him

parva rura a small country estate, a term appropriate to his Sabine farm but not to a villa at Tibur.

Odes II, xviii. This is a poem on the vanity of riches: "No ivory or gilded panel shines in my house, no beams of Hymettian marble rest on pillars quarried in Africa . . . but I am honest and have a happy talent, and, though I am poor, rich men come to visit me. I importune the gods for nothing more, nor do I beg my powerful friend for ampler possessions; I am happy and satisfied with my unrivalled Sabine farm" (*satis beatus unicis Sabinis*). The word *unicis* is translated by Wickham as "my single Sabine farm," by Professor Bennett as "my cherished Sabine farm." I humbly suggest that the word is richer of content. Horace also applied it to Augustus (Odes III, xiv). It means that the farm is the only one of its kind, unique, and also the only farm that Horace owns. This phrase, taken together with that in Odes III, i, which I have already quoted,

> Cur valle permutem Sabina
> divitias operosiores?

seems to me conclusive evidence up to that date.

Odes III, xvi, a poem on contentment, deserves a longer examination. It says:

> Crescentem sequitur cura pecuniam
> maiorumque fames. Jure perhorrui
> late conspicuum tollere verticem,
> Maecenas, equitum decus

"As money increases, care and hunger-for-more follow after. I was right, Maecenas, thou honor of the Equestrian Order, to be horrified by the idea of making myself conspicuous. . . . The more a man denies himself, so much the more will he receive from the Gods. Destitute myself, I seek the camp of men desiring naught." Next follows a metaphor, not very intelligible, of which Wickham says, "All he really means is that he would choose a modest competence in preference to great wealth." Then the poet adds: "A stream of pure water, a wood of a few acres, and confidence in my corn crop, make my lot happier, though he may not be aware of it, than that of the man who glitters in the ownership of fertile Africa. No Calabrian bees bring me honey, no wine lies mellowing for me in Laestrygonian jars, no fleeces grow thick for me in Gallic pastures; nevertheless, vexatious poverty is absent. And if I wished, Maecenas, for more you would not refuse to give it." And he ends with the words, "It is well with him to whom God with thrifty hand has given that which is enough."

As Wickham says, "The ode is on Horace's common theme, the praise of contentment and the *aurea mediocritas* of fortune." How could a man who coveted a villa at fashionable Tibur write all that?

In Odes III, xxii, the poet dedicates the pine tree that hangs over his house *imminens villae,* to the Goddess Diana, with the obvious implication that he has but one house.

And other indications here and there point to the ownership of one country place only (the words *fundus, rus, villa* seem to have been used interchangeably).

These passages put together make a strong case against the Tiburtine theory. It is true, as I have said, that some of the odes may possibly be of an earlier date than 27 B.C. although probably not; that objection, however, cannot apply to passages in the Epistles, published in 20 B.C. and certainly written within a year or two.

Epistle I, x, says:

> Fuge magna: licet sub paupere tecto
> reges et regum vita praecurrere amicos.

> Shun greatness: in a poor house one may
> Do better than kings and friends of kings.

Epistle I, xv, is addressed to his friend Vala. It was the poet's custom in cold weather to go southward, and he asks Vala about conditions and comforts in various winter resorts. He says: *Rure meo possum quidvis perferre patique*, "At my country place I can bear and endure anything," an expression that implies one country place, and he confirms this by expressing a hope *pinguis ut inde domum possim reverti*, "to return home fat and flourishing." And as to the last verse, "You are one of those whose invested wealth can be seen in handsome villas," Wickham comments, "It seems clear that there is an implied contrast between the smartness of Vala's country house in south Italy and the roughness of the poet's own humbler quarters in the Sabine valley."

To this I may add the gloss upon the ode *Fons Bandusiae* by the scholiast Acron, who lived a long time after Suetonius: *Bandusia Sabinensis agri regio est in qua Horati ager fuit*, "Bandusia is that district in the Sabine country in which Horace's country place was." Acron does not seem to have heard of any other house.

When writing to Lollius (Epis. I, xviii) Horace says: "As often as I drink of the cold water from the Digentia, what do you think, dear friend, I pray for? — May I have what I now possess or even less, may I for what remains of my life live my own master." The reference to the Digentia proves that he is talking of the Sabine farm.

In order to do the Tiburtine theory full justice, I must examine more closely one of their points. At Tibur there are the remains of a villa, known popularly for centuries, so they say, as "Horace's villa." In my description of it I follow the late G. H. Hallam, at one time fellow of St. John's College and Senior Master of Harrow School, in his little book entitled *Horace at Tibur and the Sabine Farm*. He tells of a small green valley east of the modern town and says: "Horace's house must have been in the neighborhood of this green valley: here was the Tibur of the Sibyl Albunea, and the grove of Tiburnus, here were the dripping banks, the 'fruit orchard wet with the spray of leaping cataracts.' "

These archaeological remains lie about a hundred or two hundred yards from the supposed site of the grove of Tiburnus. In this traditional house "the largest room . . . is in the form of a basilica, nearly 32 feet in width and 26 in length, besides the apse (the nymphaeum) which is fifteen feet in diameter. The walls are faced with . . . opus reticulatum." This indicates a luxurious house. Mr. Hallam also says:

It is true that Horace nowhere states in so many words that he had a villa at Tibur but . . . what can be more likely than that a villa at Tibur, like the Sabine Farm, was given by Maecenas as a reward for his great services to the Empire? Several passages in the odes suggest the offer of such a gift [we have seen what they are] and we have the direct evidence of Suetonius [cited]. It may indeed have remained the property of Maecenas. . . . Horace having free quarters there with his friend, the villa might easily have become popularly known as Horace's. We need not concern ourselves excessively as to the terms on which Horace occupied the house. What we may feel certain about is that he lived there habitually.

I have given more specific reasons for disbelieving this general hypothesis, here I will confine myself to a few doubts about some of Mr. Hallam's opinions. Why should Maecenas give Horace a villa as a reward for "his great services to the Empire"? Those services consisted of the six odes in Book III which I have examined, and they were rendered to the Emperor, not to Maecenas. Maecenas gave Horace the Sabine farm because he loved him and thought it wrong that a poet's talent should be wasted in the treasury office. He had always been ready to give the poet more than he had, and Horace always answered that he did not want anything more; why then should Maecenas give him a villa at Tibur?

Mr. Hallam, however, does not press the real motive behind his belief. He gave arguments, but the *causa causans* of his theory was that he himself had lived in that very villa, restored and rebuilt for modern occupation. I do not reproach him. How delicious to be able to say, "Here Horace sat, here he walked up and down, in that nymphaeum he recited his ode on Regulus." That argument would have prevailed with any lover of Horace.

So much for the evidence from the poems. I cannot bring a direct contradiction to confute the theorists, but the circumstantial evidence is very strong. The ownership of the villa at Tibur would have contradicted all of the poet's wise saws, would have given the lie to his preachings.

I have labored the point because I think the theory is really a stab in the back to Horace's integrity.

B

AUTHORITIES

LATIN AND GREEK TEXTS

Appian's Roman History, translated by Horace White (1913).

Cicero, Letters to Atticus, translated by E. O. Winstedt (1925).

Cicero, Letters to his Friends, translated by W. G. Williams (1927).

Horace, edited by E. C. Wickham (1904).

Horace, The Odes and Epodes, translated by C. E. Bennett (1930).

Horace, Satires, Epistles, and Ars Poetics, translated by H. R. Fairclough (1932).

Plutarch, The Parallel Lives, translated by B. Perrin (1928).

Propertius, translated by H. E. Butler (1929).

Suetonius, translated by J. C. Rolfe (1928).

CRITICISM AND COMMENTARY

Allen, B. M., *Augustus Caesar* (1937).

Boissier, Gaston, *Cicéron et ses amis* (1865).

Buchan, John, *Augustus* (1937).

Campbell, A. Y., *Horace, a new Interpretation* (1924).

Chapman, J. B., *Horace and His Poetry* (1919).

D'Alton, J. F., *Horace and His Age* (1917).

Ferrero, Gugliemo, *The Greatness and Decline of Rome* (1907).

Fowler, W. W., *Social Life at Rome in the Age of Cicero* (1908).

Frank, Tenney, *Catullus and Horace* (1928).

Gardthausen, Viktor, *Augustus und seine Zeit* (1891).

Haight, E. H., *Horace and His Art of Enjoyment* (c. 1925).

Hallam, G. H., *Horace at Tibur and the Sabine Farm* (1923).

Mackail, J. W., *Latin Literature* (1895).

Martin, Sir Theodore, *Horace* (1883).

Milman, H. H., *Life of Quintus Horatius Flaccus* (1854).

Rose, H. J., *A Handbook of Latin Literature* (1936).

Schomberg, Ralph, *Life of Maecenas* (1766).

Sellar, William, *The Roman Poets of the Augustan Age* (1891).

Showerman, Grant, *Horace and His Influence* (1922).

Tuckwell, Rev. W., *Horace* (1905).

Tyrrell, R. Y., *Latin Poetry* (1895).

Verall, A. W., *Studies Literary and Historical in the Odes of Horace* (1884).

INDEX